Dr Aparna Rao is an established criminal barrister at 5 Paper Buildings, London, specialising in complex criminal and civil fraud.

Aparna took her undergraduate degrees in Law and Science at the Australian National University in Canberra, before qualifying as a lawyer in 2009 and working as an Associate to a Justice of the High Court of Australia (the final appellate court in Australia, the equivalent of the UK Supreme Court). She taught as a Lecturer in Law at the Australian National University, and later tutored in Law at Oxford University while completing her Doctorate in Law. Her thesis focused on the bad character of the defendant in criminal trials.

In 2013, Aparna cross-qualified and was called to the Bar of England and Wales.

Aparna is frequently sought as counsel in large-scale operations involving financial, technical, or legally-complex matters. She is instructed as junior counsel in MTIC and fraud-related proceedings in the VAT Tribunal. She has been instructed by government bodies to advise on LIBOR, inquiries and Serious Fraud Office investigations, and has recently completed several large-scale operations concerning internet piracy and conspiracy to defraud. Aparna has also worked extensively on high-profile historic sex offences, drugs conspiracies, extradition, and disciplinary and regulatory work in the healthcare sector.

A Practical Guide to Bad Character Evidence for Criminal Practitioners

A Practical Guide to Bad Character Evidence for Criminal Practitioners

Aparna Rao
DPhil, MPhil, BCL (Oxon)
LLB (Hons), BSc (ANU)
Barrister (Middle Temple)

Law Brief Publishing

Published 2021 by Law Brief Publishing, an imprint of Law Brief Publishing Ltd
30 The Parks
Minehead
Somerset
TA24 8BT

www.lawbriefpublishing.com

Paperback: 978-1-913715-26-7

For my family

PREFACE

Evidence was one of the few practical law subjects I studied in law school (back in Australia many years ago). Coming on the heels of subjects like Legal Theory, Foundations of Law, and International Law, I was immediately struck by the difference in the tools needed to understand the subject. Evidential rules are largely meaningless, or at least unusable, without being grounded in the intricacies of the actual evidence. Possibly this accounts for some of the complexities that arise when practitioners try to apply the law to the facts of their specific cases. It is all very well saying that, in principle, a jury is entitled to hear evidence that establishes a propensity to commit a certain kind of offence, but how much evidence is sufficient? What if it is disputed? Who decides what propensity is established?

If you are reading this book, you will probably be aware that the answers to these questions are not straightforward.

I looked at some of these questions during three years of research on my PhD into the bad character of the defendant under the Criminal Justice Act 2003. The hundreds of Court of Appeal cases that had been generated during just six years revealed that there was perhaps more than the usual level of confusion over the meaning and implementation of the provisions.

When I came to the Bar a few years later, it quickly became apparent that the words of the statute bear little resemblance to the way bad character evidence is perceived by practitioners and judges. The Court of Appeal decisions I had studied in the abstract for several years suddenly became explicable in a wholly different light. This book is designed to share these explanations in as clear and structured a way as possible.

It would not have been possible for me even to contemplate my studies, my career or this book were it not for the unparalleled support of my family: Anton, Ananth, Valli and Aditi (and of course the tolerance of Delphi and Athena).

My thesis research owes its success to my supervisors, Colin Tapper and Peter Mirfield, authors of the leading texts on the law of Evidence, for whose guidance and patience I am especially grateful.

Heartfelt thanks go to all the lecturers, tutors, professors and other positive influences at the Australian National University and Oxford University, who helped me explore my potential and encouraged my love of research and law.

My colleagues, and our incredible clerks, at 5 Paper Buildings and at the Bar are the family I depend on for everything law-related. Several have given up their valuable time to read and comment on drafts of this book. Particular thanks must go to Carolina Bracken, Rebecca Penfold, and Andrew Johnson. All errors remaining are entirely my own.

The stated law is believed to be correct and up-to-date as at 1 December 2020. This does not include any temporary law or amendments (for example in statute, regulations, procedure rules or practice directions) resulting from responses to COVID-19. Efforts have been made to incorporate last-minute amendments effected by the (EU Exit) Regulations. Please do check for updates to the law and in particular to any rules/practice directions.

Dr Aparna Rao
December 2020

TABLE OF CASES

TABLE OF LEGISLATION

CHAPTER ONE

INTRODUCTION

A defining characteristic of the criminal law is the way in which its rules of evidence fundamentally change the facts of a case.

This is because of the unique role of the jury: it is the sole arbiter of facts, but has no say in the law that governs what evidence it is given in order to determine the facts. There are sound reasons for this. Our criminal justice system relies on transparency, consistency, and fairness being done and seen to be done. The law is often not easy to comprehend and apply. We therefore leave this task to the lawyers. The resulting factual matrix, achieved after application of the law of evidence, is used by the jury to reach a verdict.

Whether bad character evidence will be used is a question asked in all cases that are expected to proceed to trial. It is natural to draw inferences about a person from known facts or assertions. We all know how easy it is instantly to form a view about another person from a profession, hobby, mannerism or speech. But the criminal justice process relies on the making of objective assessments of another person without reference to personal prejudice.

The human ability to control prejudices and make objective assessments has often proved inadequate. Parliament has taken the view that people who determine the facts in a criminal trial need assistance in order to achieve objective assessments. Thus, the natural inclination to make inferences from evidence about a person's character is now regulated.

At common law, evidence from which inferences about the bad character of the defendant can be drawn was generally called 'similar fact evidence'. After reports from the Criminal Law Revision Committee (CLRC) in 1972 and the Law Commission in 1996 and 2001,[1] Parliament enacted

---

[1] *Evidence of Bad Character in Criminal Proceedings* (Law Com No 273, 2001).

the Criminal Justice Act 2003 Part 11 Chapter 1 ('CJA'), which came into force on 15 December 2004.

I do not intend to linger on the question of whether bad character *should* be part of the criminal trial—that is a question that has been examined elsewhere[2] and, for now, is settled by the CJA. This is a guide to when, and how, bad character evidence might be used according to ss.98-113 of the CJA.

The opening sections, 98 and 99, set the stage for bad character evidence. They define the title phrase 'bad character' and abolish the common law.

Section 100 deals with three ways in which evidence of a non-defendant's bad character may be admitted.

Section 101 sets out the circumstances in which evidence of a defendant's bad character may be admitted. The seven paragraphs are commonly known as the seven 'gateways'.

There then follow five sections, 102-106, expanding upon the five substantive gateways: (c), (d), (e), (f) and (g). These gateways are 'substantive' for the purposes of a discussion about the CJA, in contrast to gateways (a) and (b) (which require the defendant's consent).

Sections 107 and 108 deal with some specific scenarios that may arise (contaminated evidence and convictions committed when a child).

Section 109 assists in the circumstance where the bad character evidence is disputed in some way.

Sections 110 and 111 prescribe a duty to give reasons and allow for the making of rules of court.

[2] Other, important, texts have been produced in the academic context by scholars including Professor Spencer and Dr Redmayne. These will be necessary reading for those interested in the development of the law, and principled arguments for and against the use of bad character in the criminal trial.

Finally, s.112 gives definitions of certain terms used in the preceding sections.[3]

Taking its cue from the legislation itself, this book will normally use male gender-specific pronouns, relying upon the interpretive rule that these actually refer to all genders.

The task of interpreting the CJA is primarily case law based. I have prioritised giving media-neutral citations where possible.

[3] Section 113 gives effect to a Schedule of amendments concerning the armed forces, an area outside the scope of this book.

CHAPTER TWO

WHAT IS BAD CHARACTER EVIDENCE?

This Chapter deals with the different types of bad character evidence, from allegations and acquittals to cautions and foreign convictions. It examines how s.98(a) and s.109 operate, the effect of s.74 of the Police and Criminal Evidence Act 1984 ('PACE'), the meaning of relevance, and how to give notice or apply to admit bad character evidence. Good character and appropriate directions are also examined.

"*Bad character*" is defined as evidence of, or of a disposition towards, misconduct.

"98 'Bad character'

References in this Chapter to evidence of a person's 'bad character' are to evidence of, or of a disposition towards, misconduct on his part, other than evidence which—

> *(a) has to do with the alleged facts of the offence with which the defendant is charged, or*
>
> *(b) is evidence of misconduct in connection with the investigation or prosecution of that offence."*

Section 112 defines "*misconduct*" by the following closed definition: "*'misconduct' means the commission of an offence or other reprehensible behaviour.*"

In the context of gateway (g), the definition of 'character' when referring to another person's character is technically different from that of 'bad character' as defined in ss 98 and 112(1). Section 106(2) gives an exclusive, closed definition of evidence that attacks another person's character. However, in essence it is very similar to 'bad character' because it is evidence "*to the effect*" that someone has committed an offence or has behaved, or is disposed to behave, in a reprehensible way.[4]

2.1 "The Commission Of An Offence"

This is straightforward. If D has a conviction from England and Wales recorded against him on his Police National Computer record ('PNC'), this is evidence of bad character. Note that, technically speaking, the conviction is not *itself* bad character. It is *evidence of* bad character.[5]

2.1.1 Foreign Convictions

The general definition does not deal directly with foreign convictions (including Scottish, Northern Irish, and EU ones). However, in terms of gateway (d), s.103(7) explicitly contemplates the use of convictions for an offence under the law of any country outside England and Wales in the context of determining whether two offences are of the same description or category as required for s.103(2) (as to which see Chapter 4 gateway (d) discussion). Section 108(2A) performs a similar function in relation to comparing a foreign conviction incurred when the defendant was under the age of 14 (see Chapter 5).

As far as the use of foreign convictions under the other gateways and non-defendant bad character is concerned, there is limited case law. Section 103(7) and s.108(2A) provide bespoke rules for specific uses of convictions that arise in those sections. Their wording does not expressly preclude the use of foreign convictions in other ways. The definition of misconduct in s.112(1) is not restricted by jurisdiction. It is likely, therefore, that foreign convictions can be used as evidence of bad character more generally.

Caution should be exercised in terms of ascertaining the accuracy of any record of foreign convictions, and the details of the underlying facts. The onus is on the prosecution; the fact that a defendant may have been

[4] See Chapter 4 gateway (g).

[5] See *Hussain* [2008] EWCA Crim 1117 and discussion below concerning facts underlying a charge.

present for some or all of the foreign proceedings does not relieve the prosecution of its obligation to obtain suitable evidence and details of the conviction.[6] It can often be difficult to establish sufficient similarity or otherwise of a foreign conviction to a comparable offence or category of offences in England and Wales (especially for propensity-based arguments, where elements of the offending may be particularised differently). However, in *Donnelly* evidence of a French conviction which may have required a different level of knowledge or intent on the part of the defendant was still admissible under gateway (d) as showing a propensity to commit the equivalent offence in England and Wales. Note that the French conviction did not fall under s.103(4)(a) (i.e. was not in the same terms as England and Wales offence), but it qualified as "*another way*" of showing propensity under s.103(2).[7]

Questions of procedural (or even substantive) fairness in a foreign jurisdiction might trigger exclusionary provisions: see, for example, *Brooks*, concerning foreign convictions from France, Spain and Morocco.[8] If a defendant disputes a conviction, s.74(3) of PACE no longer assists in respect of non-UK convictions. As at 31 December 2020 convictions in EU Member States no longer give rise to the legal presumption that the defendant has committed that offence unless the contrary is proved: s.74(3) of PACE.[9] Presumably, EU convictions are now to be treated like any other non-UK convictions. Where there is no s.74 presumption, and the relevance of the disputed conviction might be diminished to the extent that, bearing in mind the risk of satellite litigation, it ought not to be used.[10]

In *Kordasinski*,[11] D was convicted of rape, assault by penetration, and false imprisonment (acquitted of fourth charge of kidnapping). The

---

[6] This, it is unnecessary to say, goes for all bad character evidence whether of foreign extraction or not: see *Humphris* [2005] EWCA Crim 2030.

[7] *Donnelly* [2007] EWCA Crim 3360, [15].

[8] *Brooks* [2014] EWCA Crim 562. For the exclusionary provisions see Chapter 6.

[9] For old cases on s.74 and EU convictions, see *Erhan* [2014] EWCA Crim 1523; *Zawadzka* [2016] EWCA Crim 171; *Reece* [2020] EWCA Crim 44.

[10] See *Brooks* [2014] EWCA Crim 562 re the Moroccan conviction.

[11] *Kordasinski* [2006] EWCA Crim 2984, [2007] 1 Cr App R 17.

question was whether and how D's previous convictions in Poland (2000) were admissible and then provable. The previous convictions were similar in that they were equivalent to domestic convictions for rape, threats with a weapon, and false imprisonment, of two women each in identical but separate circumstances on the same day. D accepted that the convictions established a propensity and so were admissible under gateway (d) and s.103. However, he said that he was wrongly convicted in Poland, disputing the evidence given there and the Polish criminal procedures and standards of proof. He wished to restrict the admissible evidence to the fact of the convictions only, excluding exclude any details of evidence.

The Court held that:

- The rule in *Hollington v Hewthorn*[12] no longer applies to UK[13] or foreign convictions. Section 99(1) of the CJA abolishes common law rules governing the admissibility of evidence of bad character in criminal proceedings. Section 99(2) and s.118(1) together do not preserve *Hollington v Hewthorn*.[14]

- The Polish convictions were admissible under both gateways (d) (with s.103) and (g).

- Under s.101(3) the details could not fairly have been put before the jury.

As to whether non-conviction foreign bad character can be used, the concerns expressed above as to detail, proof, and satellite litigation will normally be heightened. Their use is not, however, precluded by the wording of the legislation. In *McAllister*,[15] details of an allegation in Scotland were admissible under gateway (d) to show propensity, notwithstanding that

[12] *Hollington v Hewthorn* [1943] 1 KB 587: i.e. that a criminal conviction was not admissible as evidence that the convicted person was guilty of the offence for which he was convicted.

[13] By virtue of s.73 of PACE.

[14] *Kordasinski* [2006] EWCA Crim 2984, [2007] 1 Cr App R 17, [72].

[15] *McAllister* [2008] EWCA Crim 1544, [2009] 1 Cr App R 10.

the Scottish jury had returned a verdict of 'not proven'. In *Clifford*, the judge admitted evidence of a complaint said to have taken place in Spain.[16]

2.2 "Other Reprehensible Behaviour"

By definition, "*other reprehensible behaviour*" means non-conviction evidence.

The CJA does not elaborate on the wide variety of non-conviction incidents that might be covered by "*reprehensible behaviour*".

Examples of "*other reprehensible behaviour*" include:

- Unproved allegations.
- Cautions.
- Warnings.
- Allegations resulting in acquittals.
- A finding that a person did an act (while unfit to plead).[17]
- Statements that indicate the maker's desire or motivation to commit an illegal act: for example lyrics that refer to violent actions and weapons.[18]

The phrase invites a moral judgement that is different from simply establishing the fact of a conviction.

---

[16] *Clifford* [2014] EWCA Crim 2245, [45]. This was an appeal against sentence; the judgment does not reveal whether the admissibility of the Spain allegation was disputed.

[17] *Renda* [2005] EWCA Crim 2826, [2006] 1 Cr App R 24.

[18] *Martin* [2017] EWCA Crim 488, [24]; *Palmer* [2016] EWCA Crim 2237, [28].

As an example, in *Marsh* D was convicted of the murder of his wife (by persuading his girlfriend H to commit the murder, using a knife). H had pleaded guilty and, it appears, gave evidence at D's trial. The bad character evidence was: (i) D's interest in cutting (both of himself and others) as a form of sexual gratification (and evidence of this from former girlfriends); and (ii) in 2005 D had planned to assault someone and, as in the present case, had sought to arrange a false alibi.[19] The interest in cutting was said to be relevant to an important matter in issue: whether D had exercised controlling influence over H to persuade her to carry out the killing. The alibi evidence from 2005 was relevant to "*an issue*"—whether the murder was spontaneous or whether D had planned it and given himself an alibi.[20]

The Court said that because D made no objection at trial, all the evidence was admissible under gateway (a)[21] and did not decide whether it was actually bad character evidence. However, the Court did go on to say that the judge had made the jury aware of the relevance of the 2005 evidence and the "*cutting evidence*". He did not spell out the exact relevance of each, but it was assumed to be clear to the jury.[22]

The trial lacked explanation of the intermediate step between the use of cutting during sexual activity and the control allegedly exerted by D over H. It was not suggested that H had not consented to this activity. It appears that the relevance came from the fact of a sexual relationship, allowing pre-judgement of D and H based on their being "*sexually deviant*". The cutting was reprehensible behaviour because according to societal standards it was abnormal. It is arguable whether it was relevant to any aspect of the case.[23]

---

[19] In the judgment text the Court of Appeal (and perhaps the trial judge) cites s.100 instead of s.101: *Marsh* [2009] EWCA Crim 2696, [42].

[20] *Marsh* [2009] EWCA Crim 2696, [44].

[21] *Marsh* [2009] EWCA Crim 2696, [46].

[22] *Marsh* [2009] EWCA Crim 2696, [56]-[57].

[23] A medical report mentioned on appeal, but not admitted at trial, may have assisted.

2.2.1 Unproved Allegations

Typically, these include:

- Allegations of a similar type to the current charge, e.g. of previous incidents of domestic violence perpetrated by D against C but not charged.

- Investigations into earlier behaviour that led to the current charges, but have not been prosecuted.

- Pending prosecutions that have not yet come to trial.

- Bind-overs are a particularly grey area—they may be evidence of bad character depending on the circumstances.[24] Note the effect on a good character direction (as to which see later in this Chapter).

2.2.1.1 Satellite Litigation

There are difficulties associated with treating evidence of an unproved allegation as evidence of bad character. In particular, ascertaining the truth of the allegation (as to this see also Chapter 6 on the standard of proof) and the risk of satellite litigation, might be convincing reasons not to admit mere allegations.[25]

Satellite litigation is a common pitfall and is to be avoided. It can arise in respect of any type of bad character evidence, but is most common in relation to unproved allegations. It consists of the risk that asking the jury to use bad character evidence requires the jury first to ascertain whether the allegation is true or not. This means the jury is distracted from the offence on the indictment and is asked to conduct a second trial (the satellite litigation) of a second accusation.

---

[24] *B(E)* [2017] EWCA Crim 35, [2017] 1 Cr App R 31, [46] onwards.

[25] *Millward* [2008] EWCA Crim 644, [19].

An egregious instance of this is *O'Dowd*, where the extensive satellite litigation of three disputed allegations was a significant factor in prolonging the trial. The Court observed that:

> *"It is incumbent upon a judge considering the application to try to project forward to see the problems which might later arise in the trial as a result of the disputed bad character evidence being admitted before ruling on the application. This is because, once the evidence is admitted, unless it has been contaminated (and section 107 applies) the question is of its weight. The judge will then only have limited remedies open to deal with problems that arise thereafter."*[26]

The Court in *McKenzie* said that proof of previous alleged misconduct (i.e. not via a conviction) "*requires the trial of a collateral or satellite issue*".[27] This is undesirable and is a powerful argument against the admission of bad character evidence. Before deciding whether and how to admit it, it may be helpful to ask how much additional evidence the satellite litigation will require and how the jury is going to be directed to use it.

One exception to the satellite litigation rule is where bad character evidence is adduced by a co-defendant:

> *"We do have sympathy with the judge's observation that there is a danger that allowing evidence of this kind will give rise to satellite litigation and distract the jury and take their eye off the ball. But it seems to us that, as the rules currently operate, this is not a basis for excluding evidence of bad character when relied on by one accused against another, however desirable it may be to have a rule of that nature."*[28]

---

[26] *O'Dowd* [2009] EWCA Crim 905, [2009] 2 Cr App R 16, [60].

[27] *McKenzie* [2008] EWCA Crim 758, [23]. See Chapter 6 on standard and directions.

[28] *Apabhai* [2011] EWCA Crim 917, [40].

2.2.1.2 Charges Versus Facts Underlying A Charge

The mere fact that someone has been charged with an offence is not bad character or evidence of bad character.

In *Hussain*[29] D1 and D2 were both charged with attempted robbery from D1's workplace. D1 said that he acted under duress from D2, and relied upon an incident some eight years ago in which D2 had been involved in anincident which resulted in a death.[30] D2 was originally tried for murder, but convicted of manslaughter; that conviction was quashed and at retrial D2 pleaded to assault occasioning actual bodily harm. The prosecution successfully admitted evidence of this conviction.[31] But D1 wanted, via gateways (c) or (e), to use the *fact* that D2 had been *charged* with murder (although not convicted of it), to support the defence that he (D1) had acted under duress.

The Court stated:

- A conviction by itself is not misconduct; it is only "*excellent and very often irrefutable evidence of misconduct.*"[32] This is because it is the misconduct, not the *evidence* of misconduct, that is the bad character (an interpretation based upon the structure of the opening words of s.98). "*It is not unusual to see the concept of bad character wrongly elided with that of conviction.*"

- D2 being charged with murder is not equivalent to D2 committing an act of misconduct. Only the facts that give rise to that charge can amount to misconduct.

---

29 *Hussain* [2008] EWCA Crim 1117.

30 Previous convictions for offences of dishonesty of both defendants had already been admitted via gateway (a). The judge had also admitted, via gateway (e), evidence on behalf of D2 that a witness had seen possible drug transactions taking place at D1's workplace. Neither of these admissions was disputed on appeal.

31 Via gateway (g), because D2 had attacked the defendant's character by alleging that he supplied drugs.

32 *Hussain* [2008] EWCA Crim 1117, [13].

- In fact, "*a mere charge, unproved, could not be evidence of bad character, still less could it be bad character itself*".

- Therefore in the present case, "*the only available evidence of misconduct was evidence of a conviction for assault occasioning actual bodily harm. That was the only conviction which had resulted. It proved misconduct to that extent and no further.*"[33]

However, the *fact that being charged* with something cannot amount to bad character or evidence of bad character, should be distinguished from using evidence of the *facts that led to* the charge as evidence of bad character, which is common and accepted practice. There are many cases in which evidence of an unproved allegation, sometimes the subject of a charge, and sometimes only the subject of another person's accusation, has been permitted to be used as evidence of bad character. The distinction between the fact of the charge/trial (not bad character) and the evidence underlying it (bad character) is not always maintained: see, for example, *Hobbs*, where the bad character evidence was said to include "*the fact that D2 had been arrested for, and was awaiting trial on*" certain matters.[34] From the judgment, it does not appear that reliance was being placed on the fact of the upcoming trial. The bad character evidence was the alleged substance of the charges that D2 faced, which was said to go to propensity and credibility. The evidence was inadmissible because it did not pass the test in gateway (e) and would require satellite litigation. It was, nonetheless, bad character evidence.

The problem in *Hussain* lay in treating the fact that D2 had been *charged* as evidence of bad character. It was not evidence of bad character, which meant that the fact of the charge could be used by D1, without needing to satisfy s.101, to support his *belief* that D2 was a violent man who had a conviction for murder (however mistaken that belief might have been).

33 *Hussain* [2008] EWCA Crim 1117, [14]

34 *Hobbs* [2018] EWCA Crim 1003, [2018] 2 Cr App R (S) 36, [9].

Evidence that D2 had in the past been tried for murder might help to show that there was some foundation for D1's asserted belief.[35]

It might be argued that this approach risks the jury becoming unduly prejudiced on account of the murder allegation; exclusionary provisions may apply (see Chapter 5). Appropriate directions (Chapter 6) should be given if the evidence is nonetheless admissible.

2.2.2 Acquittals, Cautions And Warnings

Acquittals, police cautions, and police warnings are types of bad character evidence that are neither evidence of convictions nor of mere unproved allegations. All can have some characteristics of bad character evidence, but all can also be distinguished from convictions in that they are unlikely to, or cannot, lead to convictions.

2.2.2.1 Acquittals

The facts underlying charges of which a person has actually been acquitted can still be used as bad character evidence. While this may appear to undermine the effect of having been acquitted, both pre- and post-CJA case law suggest that doing so is permissible.[36] It is, however, by no means inevitable.

As an example, the hypothetical answer in *Ngyuen* was that had the defendant been tried and acquitted of certain allegations *before* the current trial, it was not likely that the facts of those allegations would have been left to the jury as evidence of propensity.[37]

Further qualification is given by *Mustapha*,[38] where D1 was convicted of murder and attempted murder occurring in April 2004. D2 had actually

---

[35] *Hussain* [2008] EWCA Crim 1117, [14]-[15]. However, the conviction was safe because the defence of duress could not properly have succeeded even if this additional piece of evidence had been before the jury.

[36] *Z* [2000] 2 AC 483, [2000] 3 All ER 385; *Al Badi* [2007] EWCA Crim 2974.

[37] *Nguyen* [2008] EWCA Crim 585, [2008] 2 Cr App R 9.

[38] *Mustapha* [2007] EWCA Crim 1702.

fired the shots, but it was alleged that D1 had been carrying the gun immediately prior to this. The judge admitted as bad character evidence the fact that D1 was allegedly seen in possession of a gun in a separate event in November 2004. It was not a gun that could have been used in the April 2004 murder. The jury were told that D1 had been tried and acquitted in June 2005 of firearms offences arising from this matter. The Court of Appeal said of the use of an acquittal:

> *"it was incumbent on the judge to direct the jury that they could only use this evidence to support the identification of [D1] if they were first sure that [D1] had been carrying a gun when seen by the police officers in November 2004 ..."*[39]

The judge attempted to prevent a descent into satellite litigation by cautioning counsel against re-litigating the bad character evidence, but later directed the jury to be "*sure it is proved*" before using that evidence. The Court of Appeal said:

> *"We have no doubt that this evidence was highly prejudicial to [D1] ... It arose out of offences of which [D1] had been acquitted. Despite, the judge at the end of his ruling indicating to counsel that he did not subscribe to the view that it was necessary to re-litigate the whole matter, in our judgment it was inevitable that it had to be re-litigated. ... It was evidence of a single incident which ... only provided weak support for the identification of [D1]. Such probative value as it had was in our judgment overshadowed by its potential prejudicial effect. For these reasons, each member of this court would have excluded the evidence under s.101(3).*
>
> *"In reaching this conclusion we recognise that this court traditionally is slow to interfere with such decisions made by trial judges. Nevertheless, we have concluded that the judge was wrong not to exclude the evidence. We add that, although the judge in his ruling made it perfectly clear that he was well aware of the need to consider s.101 (3) and s.78 of PACE in relation to the evidence, he gave no specific reasons for deciding that it should not be excluded under those*

[39] *Mustapha* [2007] EWCA Crim 1702, [38]. The Court quashed the conviction because the jury direction was inadequate, but upheld the co-defendant's conviction.

> *provisions. It seems to us that judges should be careful in all such cases specifically to express their reasons for refusing an application to exclude such evidence. In our opinion, this is particularly important where the evidence relates to a previous acquittal."*[40]

A further problem with using acquittals is the application of s.109(1): is "*the evidence*" confined to the evidence of the allegation, or does it include the evidence of the acquittal as well? The CJA does not explicitly contemplate this point, but the answer might be implied from *Hussain*: any evidence of bad character that exists in relation to the acquittal consists only of the evidence of the allegation.[41]

Separately, and not necessarily as bad character, the actual fact of the acquittal can also be put before the jury. The Court of Appeal has described it as "*a very significant fact for the jury to consider*".[42] This does appear to be a very fact-specific decision: in *McNeish*, evidence that D had been acquitted of a more serious offence in a previous trial relating to the same incident was not considered admissible.[43]

Caution should be exercised to avoid presenting the jury with a conundrum whereby they are asked to go into or behind the reasoning of a previous jury.

By inference from *Z*, a jury can also go behind an agreed basis of plea to a conviction, where that conviction and the basis have been admitted as bad character evidence.[44]

Allegations that have been considered in a civil context (such as the First-Tier Tribunal) and resolved in favour of the subject of the allegations can still be admissible as bad character evidence in criminal proceedings.[45]

---

40 *Mustapha* [2007] EWCA Crim 1702, [33]-[34].

41 *Hussain* [2008] EWCA Crim 1117.

42 *Mustapha* [2007] EWCA Crim 1702, [39].

43 *McNeish* [2015] EWCA Crim 2251.

44 *Wynes* [2014] EWCA Crim 2585, [15].

45 *Hamidi* [2010] EWCA Crim 66, [26] onwards.

2.2.2.2 Police Cautions And Warnings

Evidence underlying a police caution is evidence of bad character within the meaning of s.112(1).[46] Cautions are prime fuel for satellite litigation and should not be used routinely.

In *Pierce*, a caution admitted as bad character evidence was later "*deleted*" from the police record on application by the defendant (primarily because the defendant, having not seen the material on which the police had based their accusation, could not have made a clear and reliable admission). Since the true bad character evidence was the underlying evidence giving rise to the caution (including the defendant's admissions in interview about that evidence), and not the caution itself, the later deletion of the caution did not threaten the safety of the conviction.[47]

Penalty notices and harassment warnings are not evidence of bad character.[48] They do not "*involve an admission of culpability. It follows that, at least ordinarily, we would not see a harassment warning of itself as capable of constituting bad character evidence*". However, when what is relied upon is the "*underlying material*" rather than the *warning* itself, it may, "*depending on the facts and circumstances*", be capable of constituting bad character evidence. Naturally, this then opens up risks of satellite litigation.

A penalty notice for disorder does not imply an admission of culpability and is not bad character evidence.[49] A person accepting such a notice would not believe that he was admitting guilt in respect of any offence. In *Hamer*, therefore, the judge was correct to give the defendant a good character direction, but the penalty notice was not relevant at all and should not have been admitted in the first place. Since it had been

---

[46] *S* [2006] EWCA Crim 756, [2006] 2 Cr App R 23.

[47] *Pierce* [2020] EWCA Crim 855, [35]-[36].

[48] *Dalby* [2012] EWCA Crim 701, [22]. The complaint which formed the bad character evidence was also given by an anonymous witness, but as the defendant knew who she was, the Court held that this was no reason not to allow the evidence.

[49] *Hamer* [2010] EWCA Crim 2053, [2011] 1 Cr App R 3.

admitted, the judge should have explained the characteristics of a penalty notice.[50]

2.3 "A Disposition Towards Misconduct"

Section 98 includes the following phrase: "*References in this Chapter to evidence of a person's 'bad character' are to evidence of, or of a disposition towards, misconduct on his part*".

"*Evidence of misconduct*" has been addressed above.

What is "*evidence of* a disposition towards *misconduct*"?

The legislation does not deal with the relationship between "*propensity*"[51] and "*disposition*". Nowhere in the Act is it explained what "*propensity*" or "*disposition*" mean, and it would not be wrong for someone familiar with the English language to accord a similar meaning to each word. Those familiar with statutory interpretation, however, would expect to find a different meaning for each word.[52]

It is, as yet, unclear what the phrase "*evidence of a disposition towards misconduct*" adds to the concept of propensity.

The courts obviously consider "*propensity*" and "*disposition*" to be different, but perhaps only because they appear in different places in the Act. That is, a negative finding on s.103(1) (and thus on propensity in the two instances there) does not preclude other uses of the bad character evidence in question (which therefore still satisfies "*disposition*").

---

[50] However, the conviction was still safe in the circumstances of the case.

[51] It is a named "*matter in issue*" (s.103(1)(a) and (b)) in respect of gateway (d); s.104(1) and usage indicate it is a commonly employed argument for gateway (e) as well.

[52] If propensity and disposition were intended to have the same meaning, then by virtue of s.98 all disposition bad character evidence already has the requisite propensity to satisfy s.103(1)(a) (in so far as a propensity towards misconduct is includes a propensity to commit offences of this kind). This would make the provision ineffectual.

For a discussion of the meaning of "*propensity*", see Chapter 4 on gateway (d).

2.4 Evidence That Falls Within S.98(a)

"98 'Bad character'

References in this Chapter [referring to Pt 11 Ch 1 of the CJA] to evidence of a person's 'bad character' are to evidence of, or of a disposition towards, misconduct on his part, other than evidence which—

(a) has to do with the alleged facts of the offence with which the defendant is charged, or

(b) is evidence of misconduct in connection with the investigation or prosecution of that offence.

"99 Abolition of common law rules

(1) The common law rules governing the admissibility of evidence of bad character in criminal proceedings are abolished.

(2) Subsection (1) is subject to section 118(1) in so far as it preserves the rule under which in criminal proceedings a person's reputation is admissible for the purposes of proving his bad character."

2.4.1 What Law Applies To Evidence Under S.98(a)?

Evidence that comes within s.98(a) (and s.98(b)) is not thereby automatically admissible.

The Court held in *Apabhai* that s.99 does not abolish the common law in respect of evidence that falls within s.98(a) and (b). Thus, "*if the evidence relied on falls within either section 98(a) or (b) then the common law rules are not abolished and continue to operate.*"[53]

In *McNeill* the Court said "*it would be a sufficient working model*" to say that s.98(a) either: (1) encompasses "*evidence relating to the alleged facts of an offence which would have been admissible under the common law outside the context of bad character or propensity*"; or alternatively (2) encompasses anything "*directly relevant to the offence charged, provided ... [it is] reasonably contemporaneous with and closely associated with its alleged facts*".[54]

Importantly, s.98(a) evidence can still be a trigger for gateway (g). See Chapter 5 Gateway (g) discussion.

2.4.2 "Has To Do With"

This has been interpreted both broadly[55] and narrowly.[56] While it is tempting to begin with a simple view (the words "*has to do with*" are "*ordinary English words*"[57]) the reality is that there is a wide grey area at the boundaries of these words ("*[t]he wording of section 98(a) is notoriously difficult to understand*"[58]).

Guidance from the case law can be summarised as follows.

2.4.2.1 Temporal Nexus Usually Required

There is a strong temporal element in most cases.[59]

---

[53] *Apabhai* [2011] EWCA Crim 917, [26]. See also *Edwards and Rowlands* [2005] EWCA Crim 3244, [2006] 2 Cr App R 4, [1]; *Watson* [2006] EWCA Crim 2308, [19]; *Fox* [2009] EWCA Crim 653, [27].

[54] *McNeill* [2007] EWCA Crim 2927, [14].

[55] E.g. *Sule* [2012] EWCA Crim 1130, [2013] 1 Cr App R 3.

[56] E.g. *McNeill* [2007] EWCA Crim 2927.

[57] *Machado* [2006] EWCA Crim 837, [13]; *Lunkulu* [2015] EWCA Crim 1350, [23].

[58] *Lewis* [2008] EWCA Crim 424, [13].

[59] *Tirnaveanu* [2007] EWCA Crim 1239, [2007] 2 Cr App R 23. See also *Mullings* [2010] EWCA Crim 2820, [2011] 2 Cr App R 2; *McNeill* [2007] EWCA Crim 2927.

Evidence that is "*contemporaneous to and closely associated with the alleged facts of the offence*" falls within s.98(a).[60]

This is consistent with the original drafting of the legislation. The Law Commission intended the words in what later became s.98(a) to refer to a type of bad character evidence that would be admissible without the need for leave. It referred to such evidence as "*res gestae*": "*so inextricably linked to the facts about the offence charged, by reason of its close connection with them in time and space, that it should be automatically admissible*".[61]

In *Brummit*, the defendant was convicted of causing death by dangerous driving. Twenty minutes prior to the incident, he had had an argument and scuffle with a shop owner, following which the defendant drove away, stopped and had a physical argument with another driver, and then drove away again very quickly with the back doors open. This sequence of events was s.98(a) evidence. "*[I]t was relevant to his state of mind and might shed some light on the manner of his driving thereafter.*"[62]

In *Tirnaveanu* it was said that the application of s.98 (the whole section) is a fact-specific exercise involving the interpretation of ordinary words. The exclusion in s.98(a) needed to "*be related to evidence where there is some* nexus in time *between the offence ... charged and the evidence of misconduct which the prosecution seek to adduce*".[63] Such a nexus did not exist on the facts in that case, as the prosecution was trying to adduce evidence of misconduct on a number of other occasions. A similar outcome occurred in *Sullivan*, where evidence of past experience of committing a particular kind of crime was gateway (d) propensity evidence, not s.98(a)

---

[60] *Machado* [2006] EWCA Crim 837, [13].

[61] *Evidence of Bad Character in Criminal Proceedings* (Law Com No 273, 2001), [10.3], see also [10.6].

[62] *Brummit* [2006] EWCA Crim 1629, [8]-[9]; similarly *Bishop* [2013] EWCA Crim 2413. See also *Spittle* [2008] EWCA Crim 2537 (as far as that case concerns past convictions that form elements of the present charges, such as breaching an ASBO or driving while disqualified); *DPP v Agyemang* [2009] EWHC 1542 (Admin).

[63] *Tirnaveanu* [2007] EWCA Crim 1239, [2007] 2 Cr App R 23, [23] (emphasis added).

evidence. As the correct directions had not been given, the conviction was unsafe.[64]

Tirnaveanu does not set limits for the required nexus or reveal the period of time under examination on the facts. However, it seems obvious that evidence relating to completely separate events, as in that case, could not fall within s.98(a).

The Court applied the temporal nexus test strictly in *Mullings*. For a fuller discussion of this case see Chapter 4 gateway (d) on gang-association. In the s.98(a) context, the Court held that letters received by the defendant several months after the offence, which contained information relevant to the gangs involved, was not evidence "*to do with*" the facts of the offence. While s.98(a) is not confined to the actus reus of the offence, the evidence failed the test of temporal connection or nexus. It was merely evidence of a general disposition.[65]

Sule suggests the temporal requirement does not apply when the evidence in question is being "*relied upon as showing a motive for the index offence*".[66] This is because "*[t]he words of the statute are straightforward*" and do not include any temporal qualification.[67]

The *Sule* qualification should be confined to matters that reasonably show the genesis of the current charge; care should be taken to avoid straying into areas of disputed motive, or disputed evidence of preparatory acts, that are more properly separate events.

Thus, in *Malone*, the defendant was charged with murdering his wife. Police found in his house a document that he later admitted he had forged. It was a faked report, dated five months earlier, purporting to be from a private investigator whom D had (genuinely) employed to follow his wife.[68] The forged document was s.98(a) evidence because it showed

64 *Sullivan* [2015] EWCA Crim 1565.

65 *Mullings* [2010] EWCA Crim 2820, [2011] 2 Cr App R 2, [29]-[31].

66 *Sule* [2012] EWCA Crim 1130, [2013] 1 Cr App R 3, [11].

67 *Sule* [2012] EWCA Crim 1130, [2013] 1 Cr App R 3, [12].

68 *Malone* [2006] EWCA Crim 1860, [35].

"*evidence of matrimonial difficulties, the intensity of the effect of these difficulties on the appellant and how he dealt with them before she disappeared*". This was "*admissible as evidence going directly to show with other circumstantial evidence that he had committed the offence. As such it was capable of being evidence 'to do with the alleged facts of the case' in the same way as evidence to show a conspiracy or a joint venture would be admissible under section [98(a)].*"[69]

It might be argued that the connection is not so clear. In fact, the Court's final conclusion in *Malone* was that although the judge purported to use s.98(a), the evidence was eventually used in a propensity fashion instead. Thus, gateway (d) and s.103(1)(b) would have been satisfied. It said there was a question whether, after the wife's disappearance, the defendant was seen to lay a false trail as to what had happened to her. "*The issue was whether in relation to that conduct he was telling the truth.*"[70] This does not obviously look like s.98(a) evidence.

2.4.2.2 Elements Of The Offence Can Limit The Scope Of S.98(a)

In *Fox*, the defendant was accused of causing a child under 13 to engage in sexual activity by causing her to pose in indecent ways for photographs. The prosecution sought to prove bad character (an interest in pre-pubescent girls) via unproved allegations (the defendant's notebook and van, his behaviour towards three older girls whom he had photographed).

The Court held that the evidence was not "*to do with the alleged facts of the offence*". If it was, it would "*eliminate from the bad character provisions a great deal of evidence relating to propensity or motive. The reference in s.98(a) to the facts of the offence [is] to the actus reus. [In the present case] we are concerned with the applicant's intention and whether it was sexual—the mens rea.*"[71] This idea that the mens rea may not be ascertained from the "*facts of the offence*" but is somehow isolated from action renders much

---

[69] *Malone* [2006] EWCA Crim 1860, [48].

[70] *Malone* [2006] EWCA Crim 1860, [50]. The words 'important matter' are not used.

[71] *Fox* [2009] EWCA Crim 653, [25].

physical evidence of little use, especially in terms of using it as bad character evidence to support a disposition or tendency in the defendant.

However, see *Mullings*[72] which states that s.98(a) is not confined to the actus reus of the offence.

2.4.2.3 Limited By The Wording In The Gateways

Section 98(a) should be interpreted so as to direct evidence into the gateways, so that more evidence falls within the statutory remit than within the common law.[73]

From the point of view of the subject of the bad character evidence, it may be more desirable that the evidence falls within the statute, as then the procedure in s.100 or s.101 must be followed.

Section 98(a) generally provides an easier route to admissibility than the gateways. Therefore, the Court has taken the view that if a gateway is satisfied, it is unnecessary to consider whether s.98(a) was the correct avenue on the facts.[74]

The main confusion occurs in the overlap between s.98(a) and gateway (c): see below.[75]

---

[72] *Mullings* [2010] EWCA Crim 2820, [2011] 2 Cr App R 2, [29]. See also *IA* [2013] EWCA Crim 1308, [114].

[73] *McNeill* [2007] EWCA Crim 2927; see also *Edwards and Rowlands* [2005] EWCA Crim 3244, [2006] 2 Cr App R 4; *Wallace* [2007] EWCA Crim 1760, [2008] 1 WLR 572. In *Vehicle and Operator Services Agency v Ace Crane and Transport Ltd* [2010] EWHC 288 (Admin), previous uncharged breaches of transport regulations were "*to do with*" the present charge for breaching the same regulations. *Mullings* [2010] EWCA Crim 2820, [2011] 2 Cr App R 2, [32] attempts to narrow s.98(a) by requiring temporal nexus; see also *Saleem* [2007] EWCA Crim 1923; *Scott* [2009] EWCA Crim 2457.

[74] *Swellings* [2009] EWCA Crim 3249, [2009] 2 Cr App R (S) 30, [52].

[75] There is occasional overlap between s.98(a) and gateway (d); the other gateways tend to have less. See *Lovelock* [2007] EWCA Crim 476 (s.98(a) and not (f)); *L* [2009] EWCA Crim 2688 (gateway (e) rather than s.98(a)); *Watson* [2006] EWCA Crim 2308

2.4.2.4 Evidence Of Offences Committed By D At The Same Time

Evidence of offences committed by D at the same time as the present offence can be s.98(a) evidence. Typically, this is confined to offences to which D has pleaded guilty and which have some relevance to D's guilt in respect of the current offence.

As a matter of practice, prosecutors do not routinely seek to rely on guilty pleas to associated offences without something more.

For example, although D's guilty plea to driving a car without insurance might technically be s.98(a) evidence in respect of his trial for possessing an offensive weapon in the boot of that car, it will not normally be helpful or fair to admit it purely on this basis.

This category can also include D's conviction at trial for an offence committed at the same time as the present offence. For example, if D is convicted of count 1 at trial 1, but the jury is hung on count 2, the conviction for count 1 can be admissible at the retrial for count 2. There will usually need to be some temporal or other connection between the counts; usually, this will be satisfied by the same reasons for the counts appearing together on the indictment in the first place.[76]

In *Watson*[77] the defendant was convicted, on retrial, for the rape of his wife. At the first trial he was convicted of assault occasioning actual bodily harm against his wife arising from the same events, but the jury could not agree on the rape charge. The assault was said to have happened just before the rape and was connected with an argument the couple were having. At retrial on the rape, the evidence of the ABH conviction was admissible via s.98(a).

(s.98(a) instead of gateways (d) or (g)); *Ravjani* [2012] EWCA Crim 2519 (probably not admissible under either gateway (e) or s.98(a)).

[76] See, e.g., *Abdullah* [2019] EWCA Crim 1137.

[77] *Watson* [2006] EWCA Crim 2308.

2.4.2.5 Evidence Of Offences Committed By A Co-Defendant

D2's guilty plea to an offence which arises out of the same facts as those which give rise to D1's current trial can be admissible via s.98(a).

If D2 is now not taking part in the trial at all, s.98(a) or s.100 (*not* s.101) applies (see Chapter 3).

If D2 remains a party to the trial, s.98(a) or s.101 applies (see Chapter 4).

Section 78 of PACE may operate to exclude D2's guilty plea (see Chapter 5).

Bear in mind that D2's offence must arise out of the same facts. Thus, D2's plea to a burglary would be s.98(a) evidence if D1 was charged with the same burglary. But if D1 is charged instead with handling stolen goods from that burglary, D2's plea to committing that burglary will not necessarily be s.98(a) evidence. This is due to the temporal limitations mentioned above.

2.4.3 Section 98(a), Gateway (c) And Res Gestae

It can be difficult to distinguish between evidence that has to do with the offence (s.98(a)) and evidence that completes another, otherwise inexplicable, piece of evidence (gateway (c)).

Early on, the Court of Appeal indicated that there would be problems caused by the overlap between s.98(a) and gateway (c): "*difficult questions can arise as to whether evidence of background or motive falls to be admitted under those exclusions in s.98 or requires consideration under s.101(1)(c).*"[78]

In *Tirnaveanu* the Court of Appeal concluded that it does not matter whether s.98(a) or gateway (c) allows the use of the evidence in question, as they have no practical dissimilarity:

---

[78] *Edwards and Rowlands* [2005] EWCA Crim 3244, [2006] 2 Cr App R 4, [1](i).

> *"there is a potential overlap between evidence that has to do with the alleged facts of the offence and evidence that might be admitted through one of the gateways in section 101(1). … in relation to the example he took of prior misconduct being the reason for the commission of the offence, such evidence could be admitted either as 'to do' with the offence or as important explanatory evidence under s.101(1)(c): 'In practice nothing of any legal significance depends on which of these two routes it is by which the evidence comes in.'"*[79]

It is, nonetheless, good practice both in terms of fairness and appeal considerations, to ascertain the correct avenue so that the appropriate exclusionary provisions are applied and the jury can be properly directed on the use of the evidence.[80]

Note that s.98(a) and gateway (c) are only similar (if at all), when the evidence is actually capable of being admitted via both. In any other situation, their differences matter greatly. For example, and very obviously, if the evidence does *not* fall within s.98(a), then gateway (c) needs to be examined properly. To say that one will satisfy the situation if the other does not, is to risk ignoring the conditions that come with each.[81] It may be appropriate to say, as in *McPherson*: "*In this case we have no doubt that the evidence of the [bad character] was, in principle, admissible. Either it is evidence which is connected with the facts of the offence, or it is evidence of criminal behaviour falling within the statutory definition of bad character.*"[82] But merely being evidence of bad character within the statute does not mean that the necessary legislative conditions under a particular gateway are satisfied. The next step is to examine those conditions.

---

[79] *Tirnaveanu* [2007] EWCA Crim 1239, [2007] 2 Cr App R 23, [24], agreeing with Professor Spencer. See also *Henderson* [2010] EWCA Crim 1269, [2010] 2 Cr App R 24; *Haigh* [2010] EWCA Crim 90; *Rossi* [2009] EWCA Crim 2406.

[80] *AG* [2018] EWCA Crim 1393, [31]-[32]. Contrast the approach in *Mufty* [2017] EWCA Crim 185, [19]-[20], where neither the definition of bad character, s.98(a), nor any gateways were considered.

[81] E.g. s.102 in *Martin* [2005] EWCA Crim 3259.

[82] *McPherson* [2010] EWCA Crim 2906, [17].

Gateway (c) certainly comes with extra requirements, notably of substantial value and the impossibility or difficulty of understanding the other evidence. The breadth of s.98(a) is actually *limited* by the context provided by the gateways, notably by gateway (c):

> *"'has to do with' are words of prima facie broad application, albeit constituting a phrase that has to be construed in the overall context of the bad character provisions of the 2003 Act. Thus the breadth of the words are clearly limited by the context for instance of section 101(1)(c)'s reference to important explanatory evidence, and gateway (d)'s more general reference to important matter in issue, which taken together with section 103 relates to propensity and previous convictions."*[83]

A further complication is whether the common law of res gestae has survived s.98(a) and gateway (c), and to what extent. This necessitates an examination of the Law Commission's proposals and how they were adopted into the CJA.

The original drafting made the following distinction:[84]

- What became s.98(a) was drafted to cover evidence "*so inextricably linked to the facts about the offence charged, by reason of its close connection with them in time and space, that it should be automatically admissible*". The Law Commission intended this to refer to a type of bad character evidence that would be admissible without the need for leave. It referred to such evidence as "*res gestae*".

- A distinction was made with other evidence which, "*though not forming part of the alleged facts, is nonetheless linked to those central facts by virtue of its force in making them comprehensible.*" Such evidence, contributing to comprehension rather than merely

[83] *McNeill* [2007] EWCA Crim 2927, [14].

[84] *Evidence of Bad Character in Criminal Proceedings* (Law Com No 273, 2001), [10.3], see also [10.6].

> being inextricable, later became the subject of gateway (c) and s.100(1)(a) and *did* require a test of admissibility.

In the draft Bill, only the first type of evidence was to be considered true res gestae evidence and worthy of admission without leave.[85] But both types of evidence are still bad character evidence as defined by the CJA. As a result, the common law pertaining to both types of evidence was abolished by s.99. This would mean that the common law on res gestae as it mirrors the words of 98(a) is abolished.

2.5 Section 98(b)

By contrast to s.98(a), s.98(b) is relatively straightforward and rarely used. It is designed to apply to misconduct that is related to, but not actually part of, the offending charged. It is not confined to misconduct committed by someone acting for the prosecuting authority. It can be committed by any person, including a defendant or defence witness, or someone who does not in fact give evidence at all.

Thus, in *Apabhai*, an allegation that D2 had blackmailed D1 for money in exchange for not incriminating D1 in the upcoming trial, was admissible at D1's behest under s.98(b). In that case:

> *"The fact that the evidence demonstrates bad character is not the central feature justifying its admission. Its principal purpose is to demonstrate a motive for D2 putting the appellant in the frame, and the fact that the evidence also demonstrates bad character is incidental. For example, there may be a case where a co-defendant is alleged to bear a grudge because of some slight, real or imagined, from the defendant and this is said to explain why he is lying about the defendant. Such evidence would surely be admissible even though it does not disclose bad character by the co-defendant."*[86]

---

[85] *Evidence of Bad Character in Criminal Proceedings* (Law Com No 273, 2001), [10.3]. It may be that such evidence (for which leave was not required) was considered to be so strong as to justify its inclusion without passing further tests.

[86] *Apabhai* [2011] EWCA Crim 917, [33]. See also *Haxhiaj* [2016] EWCA Crim 83.

For an example of a situation that occurred during trial, which was not s.98(b) evidence and not admissible, see *Mahil.*[87]

Section 98(b) does not include other offences with which the defendant is charged that have arisen out of the same facts, regardless of whether D pleads guilty to those other offences or not.[88] Note that two or more offences against the same defendant are to be treated as separate offences in separate proceedings (see s.112(2)). Section 98(b) therefore does not include, for example, an offence (offence 2) of assaulting a police officer while being arrested for a different offence (offence 1). If the defendant pleads guilty to offence 2, evidence of that offence is not admissible via s.98(b) in a trial for offence 1. It may be admissible via s.98(a), or a s.101 gateway (subject to exclusionary provisions).

2.6 Procedure: Notice/Application/Objections

A party applies to admit bad character evidence under s.100.

A party gives notice of the intent to use bad character evidence under s.101.

No party needs to apply to admit bad character evidence under s.101 (unlike s.100). A party only needs to give notice (within a prescribed time period, and via s.111 and the Criminal Procedure Rules Part 21) of its intent to use bad character evidence under one of the s.101 gateways.

However, practitioners and courts overwhelmingly use the terminology of 'application' rather than that of 'notice'.

In principle, a judge can suggest that the prosecution serve a bad character application/notice, "*provided that a judge is scrupulous in not taking on the function of the prosecutor or appearing to do so. Any such suggestion to the prosecution should be carefully expressed, not least because the judge may not be aware of what has been agreed between the trial advocates.*"[89] There

[87] *Mahil* [2013] EWCA Crim 673.

[88] *Edwards* [2005] EWCA Crim 1813, [2006] 1 Cr App R 3, [43].

[89] *Omotoso* [2018] EWCA Crim 1394, [47].

would appear to be no reason why a judge cannot make a similar suggestion to the defence.

The judge has a discretion in respect of the time limits and should exercise it.[90] The fact that there is technically no power to 'refuse leave' may underlie the courts' readiness to dispense with the time period for prosecution notice. That is, courts are more prepared to exercise their discretion not to exclude because they realise that the tenor of the Act (evidenced in part by the mere 'notice' terminology) is to give more weight to the prosecution's decision to use the evidence.

For an example of an "*unacceptable delay*", see *Urushadze*. The prosecution indicated at the start of an adjourned retrial that it would be giving notice, and then gave the actual notice orally, with details of the previous convictions, very close to the end of the prosecution case.[91]

The precise time limits and requirements are currently set out in the Crim PR at rules 21.2, 21.3 and 21.4. In practice, following the forms produced on the justice.gov.uk website will ensure compliance. Key points to note are:

- The prosecutor generally has a time limit of 10 business days after a not guilty plea to serve an application or notice (in the magistrates' court for prosecutors it is 20 days in respect of a s.101 notice);

- Other parties generally must serve an application or notice within 10 business days;

- Any objection from any party must be served within 10 business days;

- Applications/notices/objections should contain at least a summary of the substantive argument being made;

---

[90] See, e.g., *Bovell and Dowds* [2005] EWCA Crim 1091, [2005] 2 Cr App R 27, [2].

[91] *Urushadze* [2008] EWCA Crim 2498, [19].

- A defendant who wants to use gateway (b) (introduce evidence of his own bad character) must at the latest give notice of this prior to the evidence being introduced (r.214(8)). While there is no mechanism to object or exclude this evidence (save perhaps a baseline rule of relevance to the trial), gateway (b) is not a 'surprise' gateway.

Under s.110 and r.21.5, a court is required to give reasons in open court when it makes a decision on s.98 (whether something is evidence of bad character), s.100, s.101, s.101(3), or s.107.

Parties are encouraged to apply/give notice with due care and detail, and judges to identify the applicable gateways and exclusions in a ruling.[92]

2.7 Section 74 Of PACE

Section 74 of PACE is not an avenue for *admitting* evidence. It is often erroneously cited as such. Its function is now confined to the provability (presentation and proof) of evidence that has *already been admitted.*

As originally enacted, s.74(1) was a test of admissibility:

> "*(1) In any proceedings the fact that a person other than the accused has been convicted of an offence by or before any court in the United Kingdom or by a Service court outside the United Kingdom shall be admissible in evidence for the purpose of proving, where to do so is relevant to any issue in those proceedings, that that person committed that offence, whether or not any other evidence of his having committed that offence is given.*"

---

[92] *PB* [2016] EWCA Crim 1462, [43]: "*Had the proper procedures been followed it is likely that the confusion that has led to this appeal would not have arisen. Further, as bad character evidence, even without a written application the judge should have identified the applicable gateway(s) of admissibility and addressed section 101(3) of the Criminal Justice Act 2003 in his ruling.*"

It was amended by the CJA[93] and now reads:

> "*(1) In any proceedings the fact that a person other than the accused has been convicted of an offence by or before any court in the United Kingdom or by a Service court outside the United Kingdom shall be admissible in evidence for the purpose of proving that that person committed that offence, where evidence of his having done so is admissible, whether or not any other evidence of his having committed that offence is given.*"

Sub-section 74(3) is a parallel provision in respect of the accused's convictions.

The phrase "*where to do so is relevant to any issue in those proceedings*" has been replaced with "*where evidence of his having done so is admissible*". Thus, admissibility is a prerequisite for the use of s.74.

Were this not the case, and convictions were rendered *admissible* by s.74, then we might be justified in questioning the purpose of s.100 and s.101 of the CJA. As it is, the legislative structure requires admissibility first (via the CJA), followed by the practical means of proving the details of the admissible evidence (via s.74). Section 74 is used to avoid the need for the jury to decide whether that offence was committed, but does not make evidence of the offence admissible.

Per the Court of Appeal in *Kordasinski* (in the context of foreign convictions, making the point that admissibility is different from provability):

> "*It is, as we have said, necessary to distinguish between admissibility and how admissible evidence may be proved. In our judgment, the Polish convictions were admissible pursuant to and subject to s.101(1)(d) and (g), and s.103 of the 2003 Act. The rule in* Hollington v Hewthorn *was abolished for criminal cases, in so far as it may ever have applied or have survived, by s.99(1) of the 2003 Act.*

[93] By the Criminal Justice Act 2003 Sch.36(5) para.85(2), having effect from 15 December 2004; further amended by (EU Exit) Regulations on 31 December 2020

The convictions were provable, as opposed to admissible, under s.7 of the 1851 Act, whose formalities were complied with in this case."[94]

2.8 Relevance

> *"Judges must have in mind that no evidence is admissible unless it is relevant to the issues in the case; and there is a duty to consider in advance all evidence that the parties propose to place before the jury."*[95]

This fundamental rule applies to all bad character evidence, regardless of whether other conditions in the CJA are satisfied.

The concept of relevance also appears in several places within the CJA provisions on bad character.

2.8.1 Definition Of 'Relevance'

Stephens' definition of 'relevant' from the *Digest of the Law of Evidence* is most often cited as the legal standard of relevance:

> *"any two facts to which ['relevant'] is applied are so related to each other that according to the common course of events one either taken by itself or in connection with other facts proves or renders probable the past, present, or future existence or non-existence of the other."*[96]

This may be summarised, for convenience, as whether fact *x* proves or renders probable, or improbable, fact *y*.

---

94 *Kordasinski* [2006] EWCA Crim 2984, [2007] 1 Cr App R 17, [72]-[73].

95 Crown Court Compendium Part I: Jury and Trial Management and Summing Up, 12.1(3). References are to the June 2018 version, accessed in 2020. See also the leading case of *Hanson* [2005] EWCA Crim 824, [2005] 2 Cr App R 21, [27].

96 Fitzjames Stephen's *Digest of the Law of Evidence* (12th edn, Macmillan 1948) art 1.

The Law Commission has said that "*[r]elevant, in this context, means having some probative value on a matter in issue in the proceedings.*"[97] There is, however, no definitive meaning of either 'relevance' or 'probative value'.

In addition to its threshold function as the keystone to admissibility of all evidence, the additional presence of relevance in gateways (d), (e) and (f) performs two further functions:

1) To direct our attention to the 'feature' of the case to which the evidence must be relevant.

    a. In the case of gateways (d) and (e), that feature is an important matter in issue between the appropriate parties.

    b. In gateway (f), the feature is the correction of a false impression—as indicated by the requirement of probative value in s.105(1)(b).

2) To establish the standard of relevance required.

    a. For gateways (d) and (f) it is simply probative value.

    b. For gateway (e), this is substantial probative value rather than just probative value (or mere relevance). "*Substantial probative value*" must mean something more than "*relevant*" and "*probative value*" in (d) and (f).[98]

While gateway (e) (and s.100(1)(b), which uses the same threshold) is perhaps looking for a logical link, the simplified wording in gateways (d) and (f) suggests the lower standard of bare relevance, rejecting any enhanced standard for admission (and, for (d), leaving prejudice to be dealt with by s.101(3) and s.103(3)).[99]

Gateways (a), (b), (c) and (g) do not contain any repeated requirement of relevance. Gateways (a) and (b) do not need it, because the feature to

---

97 *Evidence of Bad Character in Criminal Proceedings* (Law Com No 273, 2001), [5.7].

98 See Chapter 5 gateway (e).

99 As in *Woodhead* [2011] EWCA Crim 472, [23]-[24] (in the context of gateway (g)).

which the evidence is relevant will usually be accepted by the defendant,[100] and with his agreement there is no need for further safeguards of enhanced relevance. Gateway (c) implicitly requires relevance to the thing that is being explained. Gateway (g) lacks a feature to which bad character evidence has to be relevant.

In summary, therefore, relevance performs the vital function of telling us how probative evidence *x* must be to feature *y* (where the evidence is the bad character evidence, and the feature is the thing to which the evidence must be directed).

2.8.2 Section 109 Assumption Of Truth

"109 Assumption of truth in assessment of relevance or probative value

(1) Subject to subsection (2), a reference in this Chapter to the relevance or probative value of evidence is a reference to its relevance or probative value on the assumption that it is true.

(2) In assessing the relevance or probative value of an item of evidence for any purpose of this Chapter, a court need not assume that the evidence is true if it appears, on the basis of any material before the court (including any evidence it decides to hear on the matter), that no court or jury could reasonably find it to be true."

Section 112(1) states: "*'probative value', and 'relevant' (in relation to an item of evidence), are to be read in accordance with section 109*".

Section 109 is designed to deal with the situation where the bad character is disputed. The tribunal of law (as opposed to the tribunal of fact) is required to assume that the alleged bad character evidence is true (the first stage) before proceeding to the question whether the evidence satisfies a gateway of admissibility (the second stage). Eliding the two stages can result in an erroneous ruling.[101] *Dizaei* sets out the difference:

---

[100] Subject to the *Highton* principle: see Chapter 4 gateway (g).

[101] *Luckett* [2015] EWCA Crim 1050, [26]-[28].

> *"the assumption in s.109 is not determinative of the admissibility question. Rather it provides the context in which the admissibility decision falls to be made. In short, the pre-conditions to admissibility under [any gateway] are not automatically established, and, notwithstanding the evidential assumptions provided by s.109 at the admissibility stage, the bare fact of an allegation (even if assumed to be true) is not necessarily conclusive of the question whether it [passes the particular legislative test for admissibility]."*[102]

However, "*the evidential assumption in s.109 does not bind the jury, and the investigation of this evidence at trial may be liable to distract attention from the crucial issue which is whether the case against the defendant has been proved.*"[103] If the evidence is admitted, and not excluded, the jury will need to be directed as to how to treat the truth of the evidence (see Chapter 6 on directions and standard of proof).

Section 109 applies to all evidence (whether relied on by the prosecution or the defence) in respect of which an assessment of relevance or probative value is required under ss.98-113. It applies to evidence that is evidence of bad character, and thus, by implication, does not apply to evidence that falls *within* s.98(a) or s.98(b):

> *"Section 101(1) refers to evidence of a defendant's bad character and section 101(1)(e) refers to "it", namely bad character that is misconduct on the part of the appellant as defined in section 98. The reference in section 109(1) to an assumption that 'it' is true, is a reference back to bad character as defined by section 98".*[104]

The principle in s.109(2) has been described as creating a "*rebuttable*" assumption of truth.[105] There is little guidance on what would be sufficient material to justify a conclusion that no tribunal of fact could

---

102 *Dizaei* [2013] EWCA Crim 88, [2013] 1 Cr App R 31, [36].

103 *Dizaei* [2013] EWCA Crim 88, [2013] 1 Cr App R 31, [37].

104 *Mitchell* [2010] EWCA Crim 783, [17].

105 *Gabbana* [2020] EWCA Crim 1473, [44].

reasonably find the evidence to be true. In most cases, something that is so patently untrue as to satisfy s.109(2) is likely to be very obvious indeed.

In *Musone*, the Court said:

> *"Section 109 gives rise to a stark choice between either an assumption that the evidence is true or rejection of its truth on the grounds that no court or jury could reasonably find it to be true. But in reality … there will be evidence which, although capable of belief, is improbable and unlikely to be believed."*[106]

An additional condition of "*fairness*" appears to have emerged in relation to evidence relied upon by the defence, because of the absence of the exclusionary provisions that can be applied at a later stage:

> *"cases in which a breach of the procedural rules will entitle a court to exclude evidence of substantial probative value will be rare. A court should be most reluctant to exclude evidence of that quality by reason of a breach of the procedural code. Nonetheless, there will be cases, of which the instant appeal is an example, where the only way in which the court can ensure fairness is by excluding evidence, even when it reaches the quality described in section 101(1)(e). … Whilst the judge is compelled to assume the truth of such evidence for the purposes of section 101(1)(e), he need not take so extreme a view when considering whether to prevent the unfair effect of a breach of the procedural rules by excluding the evidence. The more credible the evidence, the less likely it is that the judge will exclude it on grounds of a breach of a procedural requirement. But where, as in the instant case, the evidence is improbable, the judge is entitled to take that factor into account in deciding whether to exclude it, in circumstances where the rules have been deliberately breached."*[107]

Care should be taken not to diminish the assumption because the evidence comes from a non-prosecution source. Thus, in *Luckett*, the Court emphasised that "*[i]f the allegations were true—and the assumption is that*

[106] *Musone* [2007] EWCA Crim 1237, [2007] 2 Cr App R 29, [60].

[107] *Musone* [2007] EWCA Crim 1237, [2007] 2 Cr App R 29, [60].

they were true—then they clearly had substantial probative value in the context of this case. The fact that the allegation came from [D] alone was not, of itself, a reason for refusing the application."[108]

2.8.3 If Irrelevant, Do Not Admit

The Court of Appeal periodically issues this reminder.

Thus, in the gateway (d) case of *Bullen*, the defendant was convicted of murder, having pleaded guilty to manslaughter on the basis that his intoxication negated the element of specific intent. The only matter in issue was whether the defendant had intended to kill or cause grievous bodily harm.

The prosecution argument was that the defendant's previous convictions (mainly for violent behaviour, often involving guilty pleas), were relevant to a propensity to violence "*which therefore made it more likely than might otherwise have been the case that the defendant was guilty of murder*".[109]

The Court of Appeal disagreed. The prosecution had initially intended the bad character evidence to be used in relation to a plea of self-defence, but once the defendant pleaded to manslaughter, the use of the evidence was not "*rethought or adapted*".[110] As propensity to violence was no longer an issue, the evidence was not relevant. As the defendant had pleaded guilty to manslaughter, previous convictions "*of (relatively low level) violence*"[111] were not admissible to prove the specific intent required for murder.

In a particularly clear tribute to relevance, the Court of Appeal said that despite the changes made by the CJA to render bad character evidence more readily admissible, "*the test is still relevance*". Gateway (d) requires it, as does the introductory language of s.101. The fact that propensity is

---

[108] *Luckett* [2015] EWCA Crim 1050, [27]. Compare the recent case of *A* [2020] EWCA Crim 1687.

[109] *Bullen* [2008] EWCA Crim 4, [2008] 2 Cr App R 25, [17].

[110] *Bullen* [2008] EWCA Crim 4, [2008] 2 Cr App R 25, [27].

[111] *Bullen* [2008] EWCA Crim 4, [2008] 2 Cr App R 25, [1].

always a potential matter in issue owing to s.103(1) "*should not be overstated to the extent that sight is lost of the need for relevance: the bad character must still be relevant to an 'important' issue.*" And propensity will not be a matter in issue at all where the proviso to s.103(1)(a) operates.[112] The "*safeguard*" of s.103(3) itself "*emphasises the significance of relevance's handmaiden, probative value.*"[113]

The Court of Appeal was also critical of a "*lack of focus*" in the judge's treatment of the three *Hanson* questions.[114] He failed to take properly into account the limited nature of the issue at trial—limited by the defendant's plea to manslaughter. When considering if the convictions actually established a propensity under s.103(1)(a) (question one), the judge focused only on their violent aspect. "*He added that, save in one instance, the violence was 'deliberate' but that, in our judgment, was an unsatisfactory and potentially misleading gloss, if it was intended as such, on the concept of specific intent.*"[115] The Court said that "*a propensity to commit offences of the kind charged*" is a "*deliberately broad concept, properly designed for the generality of cases, but to be handled with care when the sole issue was specific intent.*" Question two of *Hanson* presented the "*only real opportunity*" to consider relevance, since the judge

> "*nowhere asked himself the question whether the appellant having the propensity in question is, or is relevant to, an 'important' matter in issue ... [he] answered that question merely by saying that it was open to the jury to conclude that it did, after receiving a proper direction. ... if it was to be 'Yes', the judge should have explained what light in particular the previous convictions were capable of throwing on the case with which he was concerned.*"

---

[112] *Bullen* [2008] EWCA Crim 4, [2008] 2 Cr App R 25, [30]-[31]: the Court refers to the Explanatory Notes to the CJA, and distinguishes *Duggan* (*Edwards* [2005] EWCA Crim 1813, [2006] 1 Cr App R 3) where the defendant claimed he was entirely innocent and pleaded self-defence and so a propensity to violence was relevant.

[113] *Bullen* [2008] EWCA Crim 4, [2008] 2 Cr App R 25, [29].

[114] See Chapter 4 gateway (d).

[115] *Bullen* [2008] EWCA Crim 4, [2008] 2 Cr App R 25, [33].

Finally, the Court held that the judge was wrong to dismiss question three, for it seems unjust or unfair "*to rely on a raft of previous convictions which are not in themselves suggested to throw any light on the issue of intent before the jury.*"[116] This essentially restates the absence of relevance.

The errors identified in *Bullen* are not particularly unusual—it is not uncommon to fail to explain what is 'important' about the matter in issue, and to leave any uncertainties about the use of the evidence to the safety valve[117] of the jury's broad abilities.

2.9 Good Character

Good character is, at its lowest, simply an absence of bad character.

This basic good character can be distinguished from what is sometimes called *positive* good character, namely evidence of behaviour that is perceived by society as actively desirable (as opposed to a mere lack of evidence of reprehensible behaviour). Typically, such moral or social good behaviour is shown through character references[118] or evidence of charitable, voluntary, community or other public service (including certain professions[119]).

To some extent, the weight accorded to good character and the generosity of good character directions were designed to compensate for the defendant's handicaps at trial, especially his inability to testify in his own defence.[120] Since these ceased to be a concern, good character has assumed a different role. In effect, a defendant is entitled to it if he does not have a bad character.

---

[116] *Bullen* [2008] EWCA Crim 4, [2008] 2 Cr App R 25, [33].

[117] See Chapter 6.2.

[118] As to the value of these see *McChleery* [2019] EWCA Crim 2100, [19].

[119] E.g. religious employment, emergency services work, military service, etc.

[120] Historically these compensations never included the enhancement of his credibility, because prior to the Criminal Evidence Act 1898, s.1, the defendant was not allowed to testify in his own defence.

Good character evidence is usually greatly diffused, existing at a high level of generality (focusing on the entirety of the defendant's behaviour over the course of many years), whereas bad character evidence usually appears in the form of particularised instances. This leads to the result that a specific point of bad character will rebut a general account of good character, but neither a general account nor a specific instance of good character will negate a specific point of bad character. The usefulness of good character evidence is not readily assessed in the same way as that of bad character evidence.

The standard good character direction is designed for basic good character. An enhanced direction can be given where positive good character has been relied on. The essence of the direction comes from *Vye*[121] and comprises two limbs: credibility (good character is something which the jury should take into account when deciding whether they believe D's evidence) and propensity (good character may mean that D is less likely to have committed the offence with which he is charged).

The full directions are set out in the Crown Court Compendium at Part 11 and are based on the case of *Hunter.*[122]

There are five categories of good character directions set out in *Hunter.* For practical purposes, categories 3 and 5 might be seen as covering similar ground. The guiding principle for categories 2-5 is that the judge should not give absurd or meaningless directions.

In short:

1. Absolute good character. A good character direction is only compulsory where D "*has no previous convictions or cautions ... and no other reprehensible conduct alleged, admitted or proven*".[123] Failure to give a compulsory good character direction can, depending on "*the nature of the case in question*", result in a conviction being

[121] *Vye* [1993] 1 WLR 471, [1993] 97 Cr App R 134.

[122] Crown Court Compendium Part I: Jury and Trial Management and Summing Up.

[123] *Hunter* [2015] EWCA Crim 631, [2015] 2 Cr App R 9, [77] onwards.

quashed.[124] This is especially so when the central issue is credibility.

2. Effective good character. Where D has some bad character but, in effect, it is trivial and irrelevant to the case,[125] the judge can rule that D should be treated "*as a person of effective good character*" for the purposes of the case. The judgment suggests that this is not a purely discretionary exercise; the judge should consider the circumstances and fairness of the situation, and give a reasoned judgment. If so treated, D is entitled to both limbs of the direction, but, depending on the nature of his bad character, the limb(s) may be modified to "*ensure that the jury is not misled*".[126]

3. If D has bad character that he adduces solely for gateway (b) purposes (i.e. no other party relies on it as relevant to the case), the judge has a discretion to give a good character direction, which may be one or both of the limbs modified in any necessary way.

4. Where the jury is told of bad character that is only in the form of non-conviction or non-caution evidence,[127] the judge may accompany the required bad character direction with a modified good character one. This is a "*broad discretion*".

5. Where D admits non-conviction[128] reprehensible conduct that is not relied on by the Crown as probative of guilt, the judge may give a modified good character direction. This too is a broad discretion.

Other general principles:

---

[124] See *McChleery* [2019] EWCA Crim 2100, [15].

[125] Examples include old class B or C simple drug possession, strict liability road traffic or fare evasion offences, and isolated offences that attracted low-level disposals.

[126] For the interaction between a bind-over and a good character direction, see *B(E)* [2017] EWCA Crim 35, [2017] 1 Cr App R 31.

[127] These are likely to be of unproved allegations of a similar nature to the current charge.

[128] *Hunter* does not say "*no previous convictions* or cautions" as it does for category 4.

- The fact that D2 is not entitled[129] to a good character direction does not affect D1's good character direction.[130] If D1 merits a good character direction, the most that can be done is to direct the jury not to speculate about D2's character. Strategic thinking is needed here, taking into account the context of the case and how the jury might receive such a direction. It may be advisable not to draw further attention to the point.[131]

- D does not have to give evidence in order to benefit from a good character direction. However, the Compendium states that the credibility limb should not be given unless D has made some out-of-court statement upon which he relies.

Good character of a non-defendant is treated differently. The case law has recently been marshalled in *Mader*, where the Court set out the following principles in relation to prosecution witnesses:

i) Generally, "*evidence is not admissible simply to show that a prosecution witness has a good character in the sense that he or she is a generally truthful person who should be believed*".

ii) "*[E]vidence is admissible if it is relevant to an issue in the trial*" (unless excluded by one of the normal exclusionary rules of evidence; these include powers to "*refuse to admit evidence that will have an unduly prejudicial and less than probative impact upon the jury*").

iii) There is no closed list of issues to which evidence of disposition may be relevant. However, the Court gave two examples:

[129] Typically, because he has bad character that the jury does not know about.

[130] For the consequences of giving a co-defendant a good character direction that (it later transpired) was not merited, see *Broda* [2015] EWCA Crim 1000.

[131] For an example of directions given in respect of co-defendants, see *Stokes* [2018] EWCA Crim 1350.

a. "*[C]onsent in a trial involving sexual conduct is an issue to which evidence of character or disposition may be relevant.*"

b. If the defence to a crime of violence is that D was defending himself against an attack from C, "*it is apparent that the non-violent character of the latter is no less relevant as a matter of logic than that of the former*".

iv) "*If admitting evidence on the basis that it is 'issue-relevant', a trial judge should be astute to ensure that the issue to which it is relevant and its limitations are understood by the jury.*" Admitting the evidence should not "*water down the protection provided by the primary obligation upon the prosecution to prove its case and any good character direction that may be given for the defendant.*"[132]

[132] *Mader* [2018] EWCA Crim 2454, [32]-[33].

CHAPTER THREE

SECTION 100 NON-DEFENDANT BAD CHARACTER

Chapter 3 examines the ways in which a non-defendant's bad character can be admitted pursuant to s.100, and who qualifies as a non-defendant for the purposes of the bad character regime.

3.1 Statutory Provisions

"100 Non-defendant's bad character

(1) In criminal proceedings evidence of the bad character of a person other than the defendant is admissible if and only if—

(a) it is important explanatory evidence,

(b) it has substantial probative value in relation to a matter which—

(i) is a matter in issue in the proceedings, and

(ii) is of substantial importance in the context of the case as a whole, or

(c) all parties to the proceedings agree to the evidence being admissible.

(2) For the purposes of subsection (1)(a) evidence is important explanatory evidence if—

(a) without it, the court or jury would find it impossible or difficult properly to understand other evidence in the case, and

(b) its value for understanding the case as a whole is substantial.

(3) In assessing the probative value of evidence for the purposes of subsection (1)(b) the court must have regard to the following factors (and to any others it considers relevant)—

> *(a) the nature and number of the events, or other things, to which the evidence relates;*
>
> *(b) when those events or things are alleged to have happened or existed;*
>
> *(c) where—*
>
> > *(i) the evidence is evidence of a person's misconduct, and*
> >
> > *(ii) it is suggested that the evidence has probative value by reason of similarity between that misconduct and other alleged misconduct,*
>
> *the nature and extent of the similarities and the dissimilarities between each of the alleged instances of misconduct;*
>
> *(d) where—*
>
> > *(i) the evidence is evidence of a person's misconduct,*
> >
> > *(ii) it is suggested that that person is also responsible for the misconduct charged, and*
> >
> > *(iii) the identity of the person responsible for the misconduct charged is disputed,*
>
> *the extent to which the evidence shows or tends to show that the same person was responsible each time.*

(4) Except where subsection (1)(c) applies, evidence of the bad character of a person other than the defendant must not be given without leave of the court."

Section 100 only applies if s.98(a) or (b) do not. The same definition of bad character evidence applies (see Chapter 2).

3.2 Procedure

An application must be made (unless using s.100(1)(c)). Bad character evidence of a non-defendant cannot be admitted without leave of the court: s.100(4). This is in contrast to the s.101 procedure of 'notice'.

The application must be made as soon as reasonably practicable; and in any event not more than 10 business days after the prosecutor discloses material on which the application is based (if the prosecutor is not the applicant): Crim PR r.21.3(3).

There is, prima facie, no reason why a successful prosecution application to admit evidence under s.100 cannot then be subject to s.78 of PACE and the evidence excluded.

In the event that evidence of sexual behaviour falling under s.41 of the Youth Justice and Criminal Evidence Act 1991 could reasonably also be described as bad character evidence, both s.100 and s.41 need to be satisfied (see 112(3)(b)).[133] However, accusations of *false* allegations of sexual abuse by C against other persons do not fall within s.41; only s.100 would need to be satisfied.[134]

Section 109 (assumption of truth) applies equally to bad character evidence against a non-defendant. In the context of a complainant's allegedly false allegations, s.109 requires "*some material from which it could properly concluded that the complaint was false*".[135] In *Gabbai*, the judge was wrong to have excluded evidence of previous false complaints by C:

> *"In our view, this evidence was of a striking nature, and relevant as suggestive of previous false accounts. The evidence that the complainant had doubted her own past suggestions of rape … should have been admitted pursuant to s.100 CJA 2003. This provided an evidential foundation for a conclusion of falsity, of substantial*

---

133 E.g., *Smith* [2017] EWCA Crim 941, [21]-[22].

134 *Stephenson* [2006] EWCA Crim 2325; *Clarke* [2016] EWCA Crim 2030.

135 *AM* [2009] EWCA Crim 618, [22]; see also *Conn* [2018] EWCA Crim 1751; *Knight* [2013] EWCA Crim 2486.

> *importance in the case as a whole, and should have been before the jury."*[136]

> *"Had this evidence been admitted, the interpretation of the [video of the alleged rape] might very easily have been affected. As we have said, the video evidence is key as it is in apparent conflict with the account of [C]. That was properly a matter for the jury."*[137]

The lapse of time is a relevant factor: in CB, an allegation that the complainant had made a false complaint some 10 years earlier (when she was aged 12) was not admissible.[138]

Note that a person who was originally a co-defendant (D2) but has, before trial, been dealt with another way (e.g. entered an acceptable plea and awaits sentence pending the conclusion of D1's trial on the same or related charges) is *not* a co-defendant for the purposes of D1's trial.[139] Thus, an application (by prosecution or D1) to adduce evidence of D2's bad character must be made under s.100, not s.101. D2's guilty plea to offences arising out of the same facts of the offence with which D1 is charged may be admissible via s.98(a) (see Chapter 2).

There is no requirement that the subject of the bad character evidence be a witness at the trial or otherwise give evidence in any way. In *RA*, the subject of the bad character evidence, C's sister, did not give evidence in the case. The relevance of the bad character was that the sister had previously had a relationship with D, and that a number of issues arising out of that relationship may have provided evidence of a motive for C making a false accusation.[140]

---

136 *Gabbai* [2019] EWCA Crim 2287, [2020] 4 WLR 65, [59].

137 *Gabbai* [2019] EWCA Crim 2287, [2020] 4 WLR 65, [64].

138 *CB* [2020] EWCA Crim 790, [106].

139 *Jukes* [2018] EWCA Crim 176; *Bogdanovic* [2020] EWCA Crim 1229.

140 *RA* [2017] EWCA Crim 1515. Interestingly, the report of this case does not reference the relevant legislation and the judge did not give a formal ruling on the defence application.

3.3 The S.100 Gateways

There are three gateways under s.100. Each can be used by any party. The exclusionary provisions and standard of proof differ depending on which party has made the application (see Chapters 5 and 6).

3.3.1 Gateway 100(1)(a)

"(a) it is important explanatory evidence"

Gateway 100(1)(a) is equivalent to 101(1)(c): important explanatory evidence.

The definition of this in s.100(2) is the same as that in s.102 (which supplements 101(1)(c)). The broad approach to the interpretation and application of "*important explanatory evidence*" is therefore the same. See Chapter 4 gateway (c) discussion.

There are few cases clearly applying s.100(1)(a). These tend to show that applications under s.100(1)(a) are often unsuccessful.[141] One reason for this may be the absence of any exclusionary provision if the evidence is admitted at the defendant's behest. The Court of Appeal has therefore said that the risk of satellite litigation is something that a court can properly take into account in deciding whether the conditions for admissibility in s.100 have been met.[142]

A successful case is *Luckett*, where D was charged with offences of robbery and putting a person in fear of violence by harassment. Witnesses gave evidence of C's injuries on several occasions. D sought to rely on evidence that C was a drug user who had suffered his injuries during encounters with drug dealers. The Court of Appeal held that this evidence was admissible under s.100(1)(b) or, alternatively, s.100(1)(a): "*the circumstances in which he was said to be associated with persons who might want to do him harm was important explanatory evidence within section*

[141] See, e.g., *Bogdanovic* [2020] EWCA Crim 1229; *Lee* [2019] EWCA Crim 2052; *Edwards* [2018] EWCA Crim 424.

[142] *Dizaei* [2013] EWCA Crim 88, [2013] 1 Cr App R 31, [35]. For exclusionary provisions see Chapter 5.

100(1)(a)."[143] The Court reiterated that the decision on admissibility must be approached on the assumption that the bad character evidence is true (s.109).[144] The importance of the defence assertions to the defence case was such that the conviction was unsafe.

The s.100 gateways are not always clearly distinguished from each other when being used. Thus, in *Dizaei*, the wording of both (a) and (b) was amalgamated in the following explanation of (b):

> *"When it is assessing the probative value of the evidence in accordance with s.100(1)(b) and s.100(3), and consistently with s.100(2), among the factors relevant to the admissibility judgment, the court should reflect whether the admission of the evidence relating to the bad character of the witness might make it difficult for the jury to understand the remainder of the evidence, and whether its understanding of the case as a whole might be diminished. In such cases the conclusion may be that the evidence is not of substantial probative value in establishing the propensity in or lack of credit worthiness of the witness, or that the evidence is not of substantial importance in the context of the case as a whole, or both. If so, the pre-conditions to admissibility will not established."*[145]

In one of the *Renda* appeals,[146] it is unclear whether (a) or (b) was being engaged. D was charged with robbery from the till of a pub. D wanted to adduce evidence about the character of the licensee of the pub, C. The judge admitted bad character allegations concerning general till shortages and the provision of free drink, because these lent support to the allegation that any shortage in the till might be attributed to C's misconduct, rather than the alleged robbery. However, the judge refused to admit allegations that C used drugs, as the allegation that the premises were misused generally for drug offences did not help to demonstrate why or

143 *Luckett* [2015] EWCA Crim 1050, [22].

144 *Luckett* [2015] EWCA Crim 1050, [26]-[27].

145 *Dizaei* [2013] EWCA Crim 88, [2013] 1 Cr App R 31, [38].

146 *Renda* [2005] EWCA Crim 2826, [2006] 1 Cr App R 24, [57].

support the conclusion that C was or may have been inventing a fictitious crime.

3.3.2 Gateway 100(1)(b)

> *"(b) it has substantial probative value in relation to a matter which—*
>
> > *(i) is a matter in issue in the proceedings, and*
> >
> > *(ii) is of substantial importance in the context of the case as a whole"*

This gateway has common elements with s.101(1)(d) ((important) matter in issue) and s.101(1)(e) (substantial probative value). Be aware that the tests are not the same, and that the words "*matter in issue*" in 100(1)(b)(i) are not necessarily the same as "*important matter in issue*" in s.101(1)(d) and (e), when taken with the definition of "*important matter*" in s.112(1).

However, the meaning of "*substantial probative value*" is the same in s.100(1)(b)(ii) and s.101(1)(e) (see Chapter 4 gateway (e)). Note, however, that in addition to substantial probative value, s.100(1)(b)(ii) also requires that the matter in issue be of "*substantial importance in the context of the case as a whole*". There are two different "*substantial*" tests to be passed.

In *Braithwaite*, the Court gave a concise overview of how s.100(1)(b) is intended to work. To summarise the principles:[147]

1. The test of "*substantial probative value*" is not the same as the test for gateway (d). There the test is whether the evidence is "*relevant*". It is, however, the same as appears in gateway (e). "*The expression has been referred to in some quarters as importing a test of 'enhanced probative value'.*"

[147] *Braithwaite* [2010] EWCA (Crim) 1082, [2010] 2 Cr App R 18, [12]-[16].

2. The assessment is "*highly fact-sensitive*". "*It is an assessment of whether the evidence in question* substantially *goes to show (prove) the point which the applicant wishes to prove on the issue in question.*"

3. "*The issue will often, but not always, be either the propensity of the person against whom the application is made to behave in a particular way, or his credibility.*"

4. Section 100(3) contains a non-exhaustive list of factors that are relevant to assessing the probative value of the bad character evidence. These are largely self-explanatory. Paragraphs (c) and (d) primarily concern the suggestion that someone else is or may be responsible for the criminality with which D is currently charged. Thus, the factors point to the extent of any similarity to other alleged misconduct if that is said to be the source of its probative value and, "*if it be suggested that the evidence is such as shows that the non-defendant committed the offence being tried, the extent to which the totality of the evidence tends to show that the same person was responsible for both the bad character event and the offence being tried.*" Section 100(3) "*emphasises that the test of substantial probative value is a test of the force of the evidence which it is sought to adduce.*"

As noted in *Dizaei*, the considerations under s.100(2) may be incorporated into s.100(3) decisions where appropriate.[148]

Avoiding satellite litigation is relevant when assessing the question of substantial probative value.[149]

There is no statutory restriction on what kind of bad character is admissible under s.100(1)(b). The gateway is not restricted, for example, to evidence of the making of false statements:

> "*It does not follow, as we have held, that previous convictions which do not involve either the making of false statements or the giving of*

[148] *Dizaei* [2013] EWCA Crim 88, [2013] 1 Cr App R 31, [30].

[149] *King* [2015] EWCA Crim 1631, [40], [41], [55].

> *false evidence, are incapable of having substantial probative value in relation to the credibility of a non-defendant under section 100, or for that matter of a co-accused where the application is made by him under section 101(1)(e).*"[150]

Defendants should be wary of waiting for their bad character to be admitted before seeking to rely on the bad character evidence of a prosecution witness. In *Myers*, the prosecution successfully adduced D's bad character via gateway (d). D then applied to admit evidence of C's convictions, under s.100(1)(b), on the basis that C's accusations against D had been made in retaliation for D publicising C's convictions to others. D had not raised this defence before, arguing instead that C was mistaken in his identification of D as the perpetrator.

The judge refused D's application, noting that the circumstances in which the application arose indicated that there was no real matter in issue in the proceedings of substantial importance in the context of the case as a whole, such as to give to those convictions substantial probative value. The essence of the defence argument seemed to be that "*it was only fair that if the jury were to know about the appellant's convictions, then they should equally know about the complainant's convictions*".[151] This does not satisfy s.100(1)(b).

It appears that, had C's motivations been raised in the defence statement, the position may have been different.

The Court of Appeal did note that, in general, the desire not to lose his shield pre-emptively might be a good reason for D not making such an application until his own bad character had been admitted. Had there been more than a merely speculative basis for the allegation about C's motivations, the evidence may have been admissible.[152]

Bare allegations are less likely to be admissible under s.100(1)(b). In *Bovell and Dowds* the Court of Appeal said: "*we entertain considerable*

---

150 *Stephenson* [2006] EWCA Crim 2325, [27].

151 *Myers* [2010] EWCA Crim 3173, [25].

152 But see *Stapleton* [2014] EWCA Crim 1983.

doubt as to whether the mere making of an allegation is capable of being evidence within section 100(1)."[153] However, in *Lawrence*, the Court held that the complainant's credibility was in issue. Both convictions and allegations about her honesty were admissible under s.100(1)(b).[154]

In *Hussain*, C's general creditworthiness was in issue and her convictions were so numerous, varied and recent that they were of substantial probative value upon the issue of whether her accusation against D was worthy of belief. They should have been left to the jury, whose task it was to decide whether they assisted in resolving who was telling the truth.[155]

In *Moody*, the suggestion (in school records, not by way of conviction) that the complainant "*was capable of expressing racist language (more than once)*" might have been admissible as going to her credibility and motivation to accuse the defendant.[156]

In *Livesey*,[157] D was charged with drug supply offences and had been found in possession of an address book containing (amongst others) names and details of persons who had convictions of drug dealing. Those convictions were admissible under s.100(1)(b).

3.3.3 Gateway 100(1)(c)

> "*(c) all parties to the proceedings agree to the evidence being admissible.*"

This is the equivalent of s.100(1)(a). It is self-explanatory and unlikely to cause difficulty. Leave of the court is not required. Note that the agreement required is from all *parties* to the proceedings (i.e. prosecutor, and all defendants). The subject of the bad character evidence is not required

---

153 *Bovell and Dowds* [2005] EWCA Crim 1091, [2005] 2 Cr App R 27, [21]. See also *Renda* [2005] EWCA Crim 2826, [2006] 1 Cr App R 24, [46].

154 *Lawrence* [2012] EWCA Crim 2144. See very recently *A* [2020] EWCA Crim 1687.

155 *Hussain* [2015] EWCA Crim 383, [24]. C's convictions were many and varied: see [7].

156 *Moody* [2019] EWCA Crim 1222, [23].

157 *Livesey* [2019] EWCA Crim 877.

to agree. Indeed there is no statutory requirement to consult the non-defendant.

Usually, an agreed fact pursuant to s.10 of the Criminal Justice Act 1967 will be the most appropriate method.

Occasionally, the evidence can be elicited via the officer in the case or an equivalent witness who is familiar with the facts. Care should be taken to restrict the witness's answers to agreed material; inadvertently revealing more than is necessary can result in legal argument about complicated jury directions or, in severe cases, discharge of the jury. If the inadvertent material is elicited on behalf of a defendant, it could result in a prosecution application under gateway (g).

CHAPTER FOUR

SECTION 101 DEFENDANT BAD CHARACTER

Chapter 4 deals with the main focus of the bad character regime: the gateways under s.101. Each gateway is examined in turn, breaking down the elements required for each and providing a quick reference to key cases for issues that arise. There is particular focus on the substantive gateways and especially gateway (d). The Chapter looks at the meaning of often-used phrases like 'important explanatory evidence', 'important matter in issue', the application of the *Hanson* principles, 'substantial probative value', 'false impression' and 'attacks' on the character of others.

4.1 Gateway (a): S.101(1)(a)

"(a) all parties to the proceedings agree to the evidence being admissible"

As with its counterpart s.100(1)(c) (non-defendant agreed bad character), this is self-explanatory and unlikely to cause difficulty.

"*All parties*" means all defendants and the prosecution; agreement between the prosecution and the defendant whose character under discussion will not suffice.[158]

This gateway is not an invitation to distract the jury with peripheral or unnecessary detail.

Usually, an agreed fact pursuant to s.10 of the Criminal Justice Act 1967 will be the most appropriate method. The court should be informed before the agreed evidence is placed before the jury.

158 *Ferdinand* [2014] EWCA Crim 1243, [2014] 2 Cr App R 23.

The evidence can be elicited via the officer in the case or an equivalent witness who is familiar with the facts. Care should be taken to restrict the witness's answers to agreed material; inadvertently revealing more than is necessary can result in legal argument about complicated jury directions or, in severe cases, discharge of the jury. If the inadvertent material is elicited on behalf of a defendant, it could result in a prosecution application under gateway (g).

The intent behind gateways (a) and (b) is to allow bad character evidence to be used only with the defendant's consent.

However, it is clear that once a defendant agrees to let his character in, it can be used by any party for any relevant purpose with or without his consent. Defendants should also be aware that once evidence has been admitted, via any gateway, it can be used by any party for any relevant purpose (see *Highton* discussed at gateway (g) below).

In *Cundell* the defendant was convicted of soliciting someone to murder his wife. He had previously pleaded guilty to an earlier charge of soliciting the murder of his wife. While in prison for that offence, he met X, whom he asked to kill his wife. This was the subject of the present charge.

The previous conviction was admitted by consent under gateway (a). Both parties agreed it was relevant to the background of these allegations which could not be explained without reference to the conviction.[159] However the judge then gave a propensity direction in relation to the conviction. It does not appear that the defendant appreciated the effect of *Highton* here. It did not matter much in this particular case, because it is difficult not to agree with the Court of Appeal's conclusion that the conviction was safe: "*[i]t seems to us hard to imagine a case in which the previous conviction could be more relevant to 'an important matter in issue*

---

159 *Cundell* [2009] EWCA Crim 2072, [53]. Although it may be queried, by analogy with the gateway (c) argument (see later in this Chapter) whether the nature of the defendant's conviction needed to be revealed, or merely the fact that he was in prison for an unspecified crime.

between the prosecution and the defence."[160] A clearer example of propensity under gateway (d) would be hard to find.

For a similar situation in the gateway (b) context, see *Tollady*. It was taken for granted that using gateway (b) bad character evidence for a s.103(1)(a)-type purpose was unquestionably correct in the circumstances. It was not correct to use it for a s.103(1)(b)-type purpose (i.e. credibility), but because the bad character evidence had originally admitted at the defendant's own instigation, there were no adverse consequences in this case.[161] The case illustrates the caution that a defendant should use before agreeing to let his character into evidence.

4.2 Gateway (b): S.101(1)(b)

> *"(b) the evidence is adduced by the defendant himself or is given in answer to a question asked by him in cross-examination and intended to elicit it"*

Again, this is an uncontroversial provision. D is entitled to put his own character into evidence, and judges will generally allow considerable latitude in relation to the relevance of such material.

Possible reasons for using gateway (b) include:

- Showing that D has always pleaded guilty to previous offences, and therefore is truthful and willing to accept when he has done something wrong.

- Showing that D has relatively minor convictions/cautions that bear no resemblance to the current matter. This can lead to a modified good character direction: see Chapter 2.

- Drawing a distinction between D1's own character and that of a co-defendant (D2) with more serious convictions. This is a bold

---

160 *Cundell* [2009] EWCA Crim 2072, [56].

161 *Tollady* [2010] EWCA Crim 2614, [26].

move, but if the co-defendant's convictions are of such probative value that they satisfy gateway (e), D1 may wish to agree to his convictions being put into evidence via gateway (b) rather than have them ruled in under gateway (g) in retaliation for attacking D2's character.

- Placing a conviction into context (for example, if the prosecution has already successfully adduced evidence of one conviction to show a propensity).
- Showing that a witness has a motive to dislike or falsely accuse D because of his convictions.

Defendants should be cautious of using gateway (b) in such a way as to give a false impression that would trigger gateway (f).

A defendant who wants to use gateway (b) must at the latest give notice prior to the evidence being introduced (CPR r.21.4(8)). While there is no mechanism to object or exclude this evidence (save perhaps a baseline rule of relevance to the trial), gateway (b) is not a 'surprise' gateway.

As with gateway (a), defendants should also be aware that once evidence has been admitted, via any gateway, it can be used by any party for any relevant purpose (see above under gateway (a), and *Highton* discussed at gateway (g) below).

4.3 Gateway (c): S.101(1)(c)

"(c) it is important explanatory evidence"

"102 'Important explanatory evidence'

For the purposes of section 101(1)(c) evidence is important explanatory evidence if—

(a) without it, the court or jury would find it impossible or difficult properly to understand other evidence in the case, and

(b) its value for understanding the case as a whole is substantial."

4.3.1 Scope Of Application

Gateway (c) is available to any party.

For the overlap between gateway (c), s.98(a) and res gestae, see Chapter 2.

Section 102 sets a high threshold for "*important explanatory evidence*".[162]

The key question is whether other evidence already in the case is not capable of being understood and requires explanation. This is a narrow application.

In particular, care should be taken to separate it from gateway (d): "*It is not possible to dress up a failed case of gateway (d) as gateway (c)*".[163] The gateway should be "*applied cautiously where it is argued to overlap with a submitted case of propensity*".[164]

Satellite litigation (although less likely in the (c) context) should be guarded against.[165]

In *Saint*, the defendant was convicted (in 2009) of false imprisonment, two indecent assaults, and rape against C, occurring on the same night in a car park in 1989. The judge admitted bad character evidence via gateway (c) to the effect that several years later, in the mid-1990s, the defendant visited that car park at night, dressed in camouflage and with a military specification night-sight. He had demonstrated an interest in watching couples having sexual intercourse. This bad character evidence was said to explain "*other evidence*" in the case, being evidence from a

[162] *Beverley* [2006] EWCA Crim 1287, *Saint* [2010] EWCA Crim 1924, *Broome* [2012] EWCA Crim 2879.

[163] *D, P and U* [2011] EWCA Crim 1474, [2012] 1 Cr App R 8, [22].

[164] *Davis* [2008] EWCA Crim 1156, [2009] 2 Cr App R 17, [36].

[165] *Edwards and Rowlands* [2005] EWCA Crim 3244, [2006] 2 Cr App R 4, [86], and *O'Dowd* [2009] EWCA Crim 905, [2009] 2 Cr App R 16.

friend of C's who had been with her prior to the attack, that he had heard footsteps while he was with her.

The Court of Appeal disagreed:

> *"The evidence it was said to explain was the evidence, mainly from [the friend who had just left C], about footsteps [he heard when opening the car door]. That evidence was not impossible or difficult to understand. On the contrary, it was readily intelligible. Its deficiency was that the Crown could not identify the footsteps with [D]. Nor, in our view, could they readily do so by resort to the bad character evidence, not least because it all related to a time four or five years or more after 5 January 1989."*[166]

Temporally distant bad character evidence is not usually admissible under gateway (c). See Chapter 5 for a discussion of lapse of time.

One exception is where a party seeks to use background relationship evidence to explain the relationship between two parties at the time of the present charge.

In *P*, the defendant was charged with the rape of his girlfriend. The girlfriend also alleged that the defendant had on six previous occasions been violent towards her, and, on a seventh occasion, had raped her (a different rape allegation from the one on the indictment). These seven incidents were admissible under (c). It was in fact the "*nature of the defence*" that made this necessary.[167] The defendant had given his account of their

[166] *Saint* [2010] EWCA Crim 1924, [16]. In general, the lapse of time affects admissibility because of the nature of the gateway. See, e.g., *Davis* [2008] EWCA Crim 1156, [2009] 2 Cr App R 17, where evidence of 20 years ago could not possibly have any important explanatory effect on the present crime; the case of *Smith* in *Edwards and Rowlands* [2005] EWCA Crim 3244, [2006] 2 Cr App R 4, where evidence about events within a few years but not about the events charged was not admissible under gateway (c).

[167] The judge said that it would be "*unfair to the prosecution*" not to be allowed to adduce the bad character evidence: *P* [2006] EWCA Crim 2517, [7].

relationship. The complainant's account was therefore necessary before the jury could understand the relationship.[168]

It is questionable whether bad character evidence providing a "*factual backdrop*" is enough.[169]

See *Hackett*, where D was charged with a sexual assault on a particular occasion. The judge admitted evidence of a history of "*abuse and aggression*" by D towards C, under a number of gateways including (c), (d), (f), and (g). The exact basis was unclear. The Court of Appeal said:

> *"In our judgment none of this evidence should have been admitted pursuant to the gateways of section 101 of the CJA 2003 as it was irrelevant, prejudicial and such probative value as it contained was significantly outweighed by its prejudicial nature ... it is unrealistic to expect either the complainant or the appellant to have given evidence which did not include reference to the past history of the relationship, which could have included emails or verbal exchanges which took place between them. That being so, if some background evidence was to have been adduced by agreement between the Crown and the defence, there should have been identification of the limits of such evidence, which then could have been the subject of judicial management."*[170]

Care should be taken to identify and enforce the uses of the bad character evidence:

> *"In our view if a judge is minded to permit evidence to be adduced as to background evidence it is incumbent upon the judge when ruling upon admissibility, to identify the reasons for its admission, the parameters of such evidence, how it can be used, in particular what can be said by any witness as to that evidence, whether it be in*

---

[168] The relationship being a "*central issue in the case*" also meant that the evidence was admissible under gateway (d).

[169] *Lowe* [2007] EWCA Crim 3047, [13]. See also *Gillespie* [2011] EWCA Crim 3152; *Iqbal* [2006] EWCA Crim 1302; *Jalland* [2006] EWCA Crim 3336; *Kesseidou* [2005] EWCA Crim 2931; *Osbourne* [2007] EWCA Crim 481.

[170] *Hackett* [2019] EWCA Crim 983, [41]-[42].

> *examination-in-chief or the extent of any cross-examination, and in that ruling to give an indication of how the jury will subsequently be directed upon that evidence. In this case that was not done. The brief and somewhat general ruling of the judge appears to have permitted prosecuting counsel to embark upon a cross-examination, untrammelled by judicial intervention, which not only went beyond the ruling of the judge, it entered into areas of evidence which were peripheral, irrelevant and prejudicial to the defendant. Put shortly, having provided a brief and general ruling, the judge failed thereafter to provide any effective management of the use of such evidence.* [171]

If the real reason for adducing bad character evidence is to make one's case *stronger* or rebut an opposing case, then gateway (c) does not apply.

In *Beverley*, it was not disputed that there was a conspiracy to import cocaine, but the question was whether the defendant was a knowing participant. He had two previous convictions (both guilty pleas), one for possession of cannabis with intent to supply and one for simple possession of cannabis. The Court of Appeal held that the conditions in s.102 were not satisfied. Even if ignorant of the prior convictions, the jury would not have been disadvantaged in understanding any of the evidence allegedly connecting the defendant with the crime. "*The evidence was perfectly clear. It required no footnote or lexicon.*"[172] The real reason for the prosecution's desire to admit the convictions was to make it more likely that the jury would disbelieve the defendant's story. Gateway (c) is not relevant to such motives.

> *"The Crown's true position is that evidence of these convictions might make it more likely that the jury would disbelieve the appellant's account. That might or might not be the fact of the matter, but it has nothing whatever to do with the gateway at section 101(1)(c) as interpreted in section 102. There should never have been an application under section 101(1)(c) in this case nor should it have been supported here.*

---

[171] *Hackett* [2019] EWCA Crim 983, [43].

[172] *Beverley* [2006] EWCA Crim 1287, [7].

> *The gateway at section 101(1)(c) was entirely unavailable."*[173]

Thus, if the real reason for adducing the evidence is to make one's case stronger or rebut the opposite case, then gateway (c) is not available.[174]

The value of the bad character evidence for understanding the case as a whole must be substantial. The volumes of evidence admitted in *Doncaster* should be avoided where possible.[175] There, evidence of three enquiries over 17 years was admissible under gateway (c) to explain charges arising only out of the last enquiry.

Section 102 precludes the admission of bad character evidence to explain "*other evidence*" that plays a minor or peripheral role in the case.

It also precludes the admission of evidence that simply satisfies curiosity or enquiry as to the nature of the 'whole picture'. Gateway (c) cannot be used simply to fill a lacuna in the picture before the jury.[176]

Evidence associating a person with a gang can be gateway (c) evidence. In *Okokono*,[177] D was convicted of a gang-related murder, allegedly committed in retaliation for the murder of a member of his own gang 18 months earlier. D had pleaded guilty to possessing a knife, on the night of his friend's murder, at a location not far from the location of his friend's murder.

The Court of Appeal said that this conviction showed two things: that D was a party to the attack seeking to revenge the death of his friend in a gang-related feud which he may have triggered; and D's realisation that a knife or knives might be used with lethal intent if gang violence broke out. It was evidence showing the true nature and extent of the appellant's connection to the death of his friend and his affiliation to his gang.

---

173 *Beverley* [2006] EWCA Crim 1287, [7].

174 See e.g. *Iqbal* [2006] EWCA Crim 1302, but cf *P* [2006] EWCA Crim 2517.

175 *Doncaster* [2008] EWCA Crim 5.

176 *Lee* [2012] EWCA Crim 316.

177 *Okokono* [2014] EWCA Crim 2521.

Without it there was a danger that the jury would be materially misled as to the nature and significance of the appellant's connections with what had gone on.

The exact means by which the conviction was admissible was unclear. The Court eventually simply said:[178]

1) It was admissible under s.98 as highly relevant evidence of the background to the killing of the victim in the present charge, and it was therefore to do with the facts of the case.

2) It was also admissible as important explanatory evidence under s.101(c) to explain the motive for the murder namely a revenge attack.

3) It was admissible under s.101(d) to establish D's willingness to engage in gang fights, knowing that others had a propensity to use knives to lethal effect. See also gateway (d) below on gang-association evidence.

It is advisable to approach the (2) reasoning with caution. The criteria for gateway (c) still need to be satisfied. Evidence explaining a motive does not necessarily satisfy s.102(a). Lack of evidence of a motive does not mean the jury will have difficulty in understanding what the prosecution alleges (i.e. the elements of the actual offence charged). It may mean that the jury is not *convinced* of what the prosecution alleges, but that is a different problem altogether and one that is not necessarily supposed to be solved by the admission of bad character.

4.3.2 How Much Evidence Is Needed?

The existence of bad character evidence is often incidental to the purpose for which important explanatory evidence is admitted. That is, some evidence may be needed to explain principal evidence in the case, but it does not follow that any and all associated bad character evidence need

[178] *Okokono* [2014] EWCA Crim 2521, [60]

be revealed. It can be sanitised or limited so as to reduce any unnecessary prejudicial effect.[179]

There are, of course, those cases where failure to specify the bad character details might lead to undesirable jury speculation about the bowdlerised evidence. In such cases, full disclosure might be more desirable, or s.78 might provide an appropriate solution.

An example of a case that readily satisfies the need for bad character to be revealed is *Johnson*.[180] D1 was convicted of importing cocaine and cannabis, while D2 (a former girlfriend) was acquitted. At the time of the events in question, D2 had complained of common assault by D1, and the police were investigating. She later dropped the complaint. The fact of the complaint was admissible via gateway (c) because "*it gave an explanation ... for the co-accused to lie to the police that she had arrived at the depot by bus.*"[181] She lied because, as she later admitted, she did not want the police to know that D1 had driven her there; she was not meant to be with him while her complaint of common assault was investigated. This, it is suggested, is very much the sort of situation that gateway (c) is intended to remedy. Importantly, it was the *fact* of the complaint and not the alleged common assault itself that was being used, and this was made clear to the jury.

In contrast, see the selectiveness employed in *Gillhooley*, where only a few parts of the evidence in question needed to be seen by the jury in order that they might appreciate the allegations being made.[182]

In *Shiekh* the defendant was convicted in 2012 of breaching a sexual offences prevention order. The order had been made in 2005 after the

---

[179] Indeed, this can be done in relation to any presentation of bad character evidence: see *Awoyemi* [2016] EWCA Crim 668, [37].

[180] Gateway (c) would also have been appropriate in *Lewis* [2008] EWCA Crim 424, where the Court instead applied gateway (f) to bad character evidence adduced by a co-defendant.

[181] *Johnson* [2007] EWCA Crim 1651.

[182] *Gillhooley* [2012] EWCA Crim 220, [24].

defendant was convicted of rape. The judge ruled, using gateway (c),[183] that the jury should be informed of the facts of the rape so that it could understand the terms of the order, although the order already contained a reference to the conviction itself.

The Court of Appeal held that this was in error. The issues did not require the jury to know the prejudicial details of the rape conviction. They merely had to ascertain whether the defendant had infringed the terms of the order—they did not need to know why the order had been made.

> *"They may indeed have speculated about the reason for the making of the order, but that is not a proper basis for adducing evidence under gateway (c). The judge could simply have told the jury that they were not to be concerned as to the reason why the order was imposed and simply accept that it was and to decide whether or not it had been infringed."*[184]

Sanitising the evidence can actually remove the need to use the bad character regime at all.

In *Jalland*, D was convicted of murdering his wife in 2004. The bad character evidence was that the defendant had, in 1996, stolen a Montego car from his employer. The judge allowed this evidence via gateway (c). The sequence of reasoning was as follows:

(1) Found at the defendant's home were two original keys to his wife's Honda, and three other keys, none original, to the stolen Montego car.

(2) In order to explain that there was a third Honda key that his wife might have used when she disappeared (and therefore without his involvement), the defendant used the existence of the three Montego keys to show that he often got car keys cut.

(3) The prosecution wanted to rebut this by saying that the extra keys for the Montego could be explained by the fact of its theft in

[183] A gateway (d) application was rejected.

[184] *Shiekh* [2013] EWCA Crim 907, [9].

1996. In interview, when asked "*how did you manage to steal the Montego?*", the defendant replied: "*I had the keys, spare keys cut*".

The Court of Appeal said that this was not evidence worthy of gateway (c). "*It is difficult to see how the fact that the Montego was stolen truly explains why three sets of keys to it existed.*"[185] The "*patent irrelevance of stealing a car in 1996 to a charge of murdering one's wife in 2004*" was "*an irrelevance which any jury would have appreciated*".[186] If anything needed to be explained so that the jury could properly understand the existence of non-original keys, it would have been the dates and frequency of the defendant's obtaining such keys, not the motive. Thus, the bad character could be removed from the important explanatory evidence. This would, in fact, render the evidence wholly exempt from the CJA scheme for bad character evidence.

Thus, the relevance of bad character in gateway (c) is actually very limited because the existence of the bad character is incidental to the primary purpose of explanation. It is not being introduced in order to show the bad character itself, unlike gateways (d), (e), (f) and (g). Wherever possible, the bad character should be removed from the admissible evidence where it does not contribute to the reason why evidence X needs explanation. Only where the explanatory evidence happens to be inextricable from bad character evidence should that bad character evidence be admitted.

4.4 Gateway (d): S.101(1)(d)

"(d) it is relevant to an important matter in issue between the defendant and the prosecution"

"103 'Matter in issue between the defendant and the prosecution'

(1) For the purposes of section 101(1)(d) the matters in issue between the defendant and the prosecution include—

---

[185] *Jalland* [2006] EWCA Crim 3336, [25].

[186] *Jalland* [2006] EWCA Crim 3336, [29].

(a) the question whether the defendant has a propensity to commit offences of the kind with which he is charged, except where his having such a propensity makes it no more likely that he is guilty of the offence;

(b) the question whether the defendant has a propensity to be untruthful, except where it is not suggested that the defendant's case is untruthful in any respect.

(2) Where subsection (1)(a) applies, a defendant's propensity to commit offences of the kind with which he is charged may (without prejudice to any other way of doing so) be established by evidence that he has been convicted of—

(a) an offence of the same description as the one with which he is charged, or

(b) an offence of the same category as the one with which he is charged.

(3) Subsection (2) does not apply in the case of a particular defendant if the court is satisfied, by reason of the length of time since the conviction or for any other reason, that it would be unjust for it to apply in his case.

(4) For the purposes of subsection (2)—

(a) two offences are of the same description as each other if the statement of the offence in a written charge or indictment would, in each case, be in the same terms;

(b) two offences are of the same category as each other if they belong to the same category of offences prescribed for the purposes of this section by an order made by the Secretary of State.

(5) A category prescribed by an order under subsection (4)(b) must consist of offences of the same type.

(6) Only prosecution evidence is admissible under section 101(1)(d).

(7) Where—

(a) a defendant has been convicted of an offence under the law of any country outside England and Wales ('the previous offence'), and

(b) the previous offence would constitute an offence under the law of England and Wales ('the corresponding offence') if it were done in England and Wales at the time of the trial for the offence with which the defendant is now charged ('the current offence'),

subsection (8) applies for the purpose of determining if the previous offence and the current offence are of the same description or category.

(8) For the purposes of subsection (2)—

(a) the previous offence is of the same description as the current offence if the corresponding offence is of that same description, as set out in subsection (4)(a);

(b) the previous offence is of the same category as the current offence if the current offence and the corresponding offence belong to the same category of offences prescribed as mentioned in subsection (4)(b)."

[Sub-sections (9), (10) and (11) concern foreign service offences]

4.4.1 The Elements Of Gateway (d)

It can help to approach gateway (d) by breaking down the elements as follows:

1. Identify what kind of bad character evidence it is (i.e. conviction, allegation etc, see Chapter 2.1 and 2.2).

2. Identify an important matter in issue between D and P (see below).

3. Identify how the bad character evidence is relevant to that matter in issue (see Chapter 2.8).

4. Identify any exclusions (see Chapter 5).

4.4.2 How To Use Gateway (d)

The prosecution should not routinely make applications to adduce bad character evidence.[187] A prosecution decision to use bad character evidence should be made on the basis of its usefulness in the case, not because the defendant has or may have a bad character.

Gateway (d) is frequently used for evidence that is relied upon to show a propensity. Propensity is not, however, the only reason for using gateway (d): see the full discussion of possible "*matters in issue*" below.

For situations where gateway (d) and s.103(1)(a) are invoked, the three questions in *Hanson* essentially present, in a different way, the requirements of, specifically, s.103(1)(a), s.103(2), s.103(3) and s.101(3). These three questions are:[188]

> 1. Does the history of conviction(s) establish a propensity to commit offences of the kind charged?
>
> 2. Does that propensity make it more likely that the defendant committed the offence charged?
>
> 3. Is it unjust to rely on the conviction(s) of the same description or category; and, in any event, will the proceedings be unfair if they are admitted?

The *Hanson* questions are not a substitute for following the full requirements of gateway (d).

Crucially, the questions do not include the gateway requirement of relevance to an important matter in issue.

Further, the questions do not cover all the possibilities that s.103(1)(a) invites: s.103(2) "*is not exhaustive of the types of conviction which might be relied upon to show evidence of propensity to commit offences of the kind*

[187] *Hanson* [2005] EWCA Crim 824, [2005] 2 Cr App R 21, [4].

[188] *Hanson* [2005] EWCA Crim 824, [2005] 2 Cr App R 21, [7].

charged", nor does merely having a conviction that is of the same description or category automatically show propensity.[189]

The third question cannot limit the application of s.101(3)[190] to the use of convictions of the same description or category. Clearly s.101(3) applies to all forms of bad character evidence (convictions of any category or otherwise, and non-conviction evidence).

Hanson then goes on to make a number of well-known statements about the nature of convictions that are capable of proving propensity in the s.103(1)(a) context.

In brief, these are:

i) Striking similarity is not needed[191] (but a degree of similarity is[192]).

ii) Any number of events may demonstrate a propensity, but in general, fewer convictions provide weaker evidence of propensity. A single conviction of sufficient distinctiveness may in some circumstances be sufficient.[193]

iii) Both s.101(3) and s.103(3) should be considered. Section 101(3) can be influenced by the degree of

[189] *Hanson* [2005] EWCA Crim 824, [2005] 2 Cr App R 21, [8].

[190] As opposed to s.103(3).

[191] *Hanson* [2005] EWCA Crim 824, [2005] 2 Cr App R 21, [9]; *Jackson* [2011] EWCA Crim 1870, [32]; *Dossett* [2013] EWCA Crim 710, [28]. Although a few cases, e.g. *Brisland* [2008] EWCA Crim 2773, [13], have still referred to it.

[192] *Hassan* [2007] EWCA Crim 1287, [26]; *Jackson* [2011] EWCA Crim 1870, [34] refers to "*circumstances … sufficiently similar to bring probative significance to the previous conviction*".

[193] *Hanson* [2005] EWCA Crim 824, [2005] 2 Cr App R 21, [9]. For single conviction not sufficient see *Khan* [2020] EWCA Crim 163; *McGarvie* [2011] EWCA Crim 1414; *Benabbou* [2012] EWCA Crim 1256; *O'Dowd* [2009] EWCA Crim 905, [2009] 2 Cr App R 16. For examples of sufficient single convictions: *Day* [2019] EWCA Crim 935; *Spottiswood* [2019] EWCA Crim 949; *Hay* [2017] EWCA Crim 1851; *Larkin* [2016] EWCA Crim 170; *Brown* [2012] EWCA Crim 773.

similarity between the previous conviction and the offence charge. Section 103(3) can be influenced by the strength of the prosecution case.[194]

iv) Old convictions are generally of less assistance and, if used, are more likely to result in unfairness.[195]

v) Propensity to untruthfulness is not the same as propensity to dishonesty. Convictions assist on s.103(1)(b) only if they show untruthfulness in some way and truthfulness is in issue.[196]

vi) Bad character evidence (not just conviction-evidence) cannot be used to bolster a weak case or prejudice the jury against the defendant.[197] As to this see more below.

vii) Parties need to co-operate in establishing the facts of previous convictions, and in some cases more detailed facts will be needed.[198]

---

194 *Hanson* [2005] EWCA Crim 824, [2005] 2 Cr App R 21, [10]; see also *De Vos* [2006] EWCA Crim 1688; *DPP v Chand* [2007] EWHC 90 (Admin); *Thomas* [2010] EWCA Crim 148.

195 *Hanson* [2005] EWCA Crim 824, [2005] 2 Cr App R 21, [11]; *Murphy* [2006] EWCA Crim 3408.

196 *Hanson* [2005] EWCA Crim 824, [2005] 2 Cr App R 21, [13]. See also *Purcell* [2006] EWCA Crim 1264; *Burns* [2006] EWCA Crim 617; *Campbell* [2007] EWCA Crim 1472, [2007] 2 Cr App R 28; *Edwards* [2005] EWCA Crim 1813, [2006] 1 Cr App R 3; *Alobaydi* [2007] EWCA Crim 145; *Garnham* [2008] EWCA Crim 266; cf *Stephenson* [2006] EWCA Crim 2325 (non-defendant); *Clarke* [2011] EWCA Crim 939 (gateway (g)).

197 *Hanson* [2005] EWCA Crim 824, [2005] 2 Cr App R 21, [18].

198 *Hanson* [2005] EWCA Crim 824, [2005] 2 Cr App R 21, [17]; *Steen* [2007] EWCA Crim 335, [2008] 2 Cr App R 26. When bad character evidence is in the form of a conviction, there are sometimes problems in proving the fact of conviction or the facts underlying the conviction. This rarely seems to be an obstacle to their ultimate admissibility. For usage of s.74(3) PACE see *C* [2010] EWCA Crim 2971, [2011] 1 WLR 1942.

viii) The Court of Appeal will only interfere with a judge's decision on bad character evidence in quite limited circumstances.[199]

Hanson is not limited to the use of bad character evidence in the form of convictions used only to show propensity to commit a type of offence. It also covers s.103(1)(b).

The judgment indicates that the observations in relation to s.103(1)(a) can be used in other contexts as well.[200]

Further, it makes a number of statements (about notice, jury warnings, establishing facts, satellite litigation) that are of use in relation to any consideration of s.101 evidence.

4.4.2.1 Satellite litigation

In particular, satellite litigation is should be avoided. This is the risk that the tribunal of fact will be tempted to 'try' the bad character allegation in an attempt to ascertain its appropriate role in the main question of guilt. Doing so can result in a 'satellite trial' of the bad character allegation, which the Court has cautioned against.[201] Moreover, the current trial is not intended to try the guilt of the defendant in other matters, and the full evidence necessary for a fair trial of those matters is usually unavailable.

The Court in *McKenzie* adopts several useful principles from *Hanson*:

---

[199] *Hanson* [2005] EWCA Crim 824, [2005] 2 Cr App R 21, [15]; see e.g. *Edwards and Rowlands* [2005] EWCA Crim 3244, [2006] 2 Cr App R 4, also *Renda* [2005] EWCA Crim 2826, [2006] 1 Cr App R 24, where one of the limits on interference is deference to the judge's "*feel*" for the case.

[200] As, e.g., *Hanson* [2005] EWCA Crim 824, [2005] 2 Cr App R 21, [13] about the number of convictions in relation to both s.103(1)(a) and (b).

[201] See also *Bovell and Dowds* [2005] EWCA Crim 1091, [2005] 2 Cr App R 27; *M* [2006] EWCA Crim 1509; *O'Dowd* [2009] EWCA Crim 905, [2009] 2 Cr App R 16; *Dalby* [2012] EWCA Crim 701, [25].

> *"A single previous conviction is unlikely to show propensity unless it shows a tendency to unusual behaviour or where the particular circumstances demonstrate probative force in relation to the offence charged. The same comments apply to allegations of past misconduct, but here a dilemma arises. If the allegations of previous misconduct are few in number, they may well fail to show propensity even if they are true, but the greater the plethora of collateral allegations, the greater the risk of the trial losing its proper focus."*[202]

An example of sufficiently unusual behaviour is contained in *Spottiswood*: a previous conviction from seven years earlier, where the defendant used a headlock in a particular way, was "*highly distinctive behaviour when carrying out an attack*".[203]

4.4.2.2 Bolstering a weak case

There are few cases explicitly applying this principle with success. *Hanson* expressed it thus: "*Evidence of bad character cannot be used simply to bolster a weak case, or to prejudice the minds of a jury against a defendant.*" The idea is that the prosecution should not take unfair advantage of a defendant's bad character to plug gaps in the integrity of its case.

While *Hanson* does not expressly say that bad character evidence is *inadmissible* if the prosecution case is weak, the practical effect is that if a case is weak, there is no permissible use the jury can make of the bad character evidence. It is therefore for most practical purposes inadmissible. In some limited cases it may be logical to admit the evidence but direct the jury that if they consider the prosecution case is otherwise weak, they cannot rely on the bad character evidence. This would be an enhanced version of the standard direction that "*D's previous convictions may only be used as*

---

202 *McKenzie* [2008] EWCA Crim 758, [24]; but see the failure to deal with the complication of satellite issues in *Gumbrell* [2009] EWCA Crim 550, [23].

203 *Spottiswood* [2019] EWCA Crim 949, [32]. See also *Bryon* [2015] EWCA Crim 997, involving an unusual method of commercial burglary.

some support for the prosecution case. You must not convict D wholly or mainly because of them."

The Court of Appeal has tended to equate the strength of the prosecution case with whether there is any separate plausible evidence linking the defendant to the crime. It is often akin to the 'no case to answer' criteria:

> *"We note that—realistically—the defence made no submission to the judge that there was no case to answer. That is not, of course, conclusive but we consider that it reflects the fact that the case against the defendant, although partly circumstantial, was well above the Plimsoll line of a weak case below which previous convictions should not be admitted."*[204]

In *Killick*, the judge rightly excluded bad character evidence under s.101(3) because it was evidence with which the prosecution sought to bolster a weak case (that D had committed a commercial burglary). The judge correctly went on to accede to an application of no case to answer. The bad character evidence consisted of statements made in interview to the effect that D was a drug user who had a drug debt. The prosecution case depended upon D's DNA being found on a moveable item at the scene of the burglary. The prosecution's reliance on D's partner, whose evidence now provided a possible alibi, left the prosecution in an "*inconsistent position*".[205]

Another successful case is *K*, where the wrongful admission of hearsay evidence meant that the subsequent admission of bad character evidence was actually made against the background of a weak prosecution case.[206] This is an unusual concatenation of circumstances.

[204] *Stanley* [2016] EWCA Crim 1801, [15].

[205] *Killick* [2020] EWCA Crim 785.

[206] *K* [2012] EWCA Crim 2943.

In *Richards*, while defence counsel came closer than most in his submission "*with force that the evidence was, in reality, used to bolster a weak case*", the Court did not actually decide whether the case was weak or not.[207]

In *DPP v Chand*, the judge concluded that the bad character evidence was admissible under gateway (d), but excluded it under s.101(3) because in his judgment the prosecution case was not strong.[208]

The weakness or otherwise of the prosecution case is generally one for the reasonable exercise of the judge's discretion.[209]

In *Hamidi*, the Court did express concern that the judge's direction had suggested that the jury might, but for the bad character evidence, regard the prosecution case against the defendant as "*unconvincing*". It could be said that the judge was inviting the jury to treat the evidence as sufficient to bolster a weak case.

> *"We have been troubled by this submission. We recognise that the terms in which the Judge expressed himself were capable of giving that impression to the jury. We have to consider whether the jury may reasonably have so understood him. ... In these circumstances, we do not consider that the jury could have misunderstood the Judge's intention, namely to point out that if they found that the appellant had participated knowledgably [in the bad character allegation] that was capable of being important evidence going to the issue of knowledge during his participation in the [current charge]. The Judge was not saying and could not reasonably be understood as saying that previous participation in [the earlier alleged fraud] was conclusive. The jury had been specifically directed to the contrary."*[210]

[207] *Richards* [2018] EWCA Crim 2374, [91].

[208] *DPP v Chand* [2007] EWHC 90 (Admin).

[209] *Powell* [2015] EWCA Crim 2200, [14]; *LN* [2014] EWCA Crim 506; *McDonald* [2007] EWCA Crim 1194.

[210] *Hamidi* [2010] EWCA Crim 66, [38].

It can be useful to defer the decision on the weakness or strength of the prosecution case until the evidence has been heard, especially in cases relying on circumstantial evidence.[211]

4.4.3 What Is Propensity?

The Court of Appeal has regularly examined what "*propensity*" means. There is no unified result. There are countless examples of what propensity means in the context of specific cases. These are of limited use unless one comes across a case that is sufficiently similar to the current case.

As far as useful guiding principles for daily application go, the following may assist.

- Apply *Hanson* above as to propensity and s.103(1).
- Propensity is, at most, an incidental issue. The most important evidence is that which bears directly on the defendant's guilt or innocence. Propensity cannot alone establish guilt and it must not be regarded as a satisfactory substitute for direct evidence of the accused's involvement in the crime charged.[212]
- Excessive recourse to cumulative past incidents may skew the trial in a way which distracts attention from the central issue. This is so even if the past incidents are undoubtedly helpful.[213]
- An adverse effect can arise through the sheer weight of disputed evidence on other uncharged allegations.[214] In such cases s.101(3) should be employed.

---

[211] *Lewis* [2014] EWCA Crim 48, [2014] 2 Cr App R (S) 27, [115]-[117].

[212] *Mitchell* [2016] UKSC 55, [2017] AC 571, [55].

[213] *Mitchell* [2016] UKSC 55, [2017] AC 571, [53].

[214] *Mitchell* [2016] UKSC 55, [2017] AC 571, [53].

- Minimise terminology that is not in the legislation or pre-dates the legislation. This includes 'striking similarity', 'similar fact' and 'tendency'.[215]

- Propensity is not "*disposition*" —this means something different in the CJA.[216] Looking for "*disposition*" is largely unhelpful.

- Convictions are not admissible if they merely show a preparedness to engage in crime of "*vaguely the same kind*" as the current offence. "*There must be a logical basis for concluding that the previous offending shows that the defendant was more likely to be prepared to commit the specific crime in question. Provided such a logical connection can be made, there is no requirement that the previous offending should consist of or include an offence of a strikingly, or even markedly closely, similar nature to the index offence.*"[217]

- When "*propensity*" bad character evidence is relied upon, bootstrapping is not allowed. See Chapter 6 on cross-admissibility. Thus, if incident A is relied upon as propensity, the jury must be sure of incident A before being permitted to use it as propensity towards the current charge. The jury cannot use the evidence in its entirety (including that of the current charge) to be satisfied of the truth of incident A, and then use incident A as support for the current charge. This is in contrast to the situation where several instances of "*coincidence*" bad character are relied on to form a propensity. Here, the jury should consider the evidence cumulatively, not separately.[218]

---

[215] In 2012 the Court of Appeal, rather than using the legislative terminology of 'bad character evidence', referred instead to "*the admissibility of what may loosely be called 'similar fact' evidence under section 101(1)(c) and (d) CJA*": *Suleman* [2012] EWCA Crim 1569, [2012] 2 Cr App R 30, [4].

[216] See Chapter 2.

[217] *Dossett* [2013] EWCA Crim 710, [28].

[218] *Mitchell* [2016] UKSC 55, [2017] AC 571, [49].

- For the standard of proof to be applied to propensity evidence, see Chapter 6.

It is notable that cases use slightly different phrases for encapsulating what propensity evidence is, and none has been decisively adopted as a definition or test.

Subsections 103(2) and (4) set out specific instances in which propensity might more readily be established. The language is permissive but not mandatory ("*may*"). The usefulness of s.103(2) is in practice extremely limited. It is not an alternative route to admissibility and is not an invitation to admit all convictions of the same category or description regardless of their probative effect. Merely being of the same description or the same category does not automatically make convictions admissible.[219] It simply provides one means by which propensity can be identified. The test of relevance (or "*probative force*"[220]) must still be satisfied for each piece of bad character evidence.

Section 103(2) applies only to convictions. Other items of bad character evidence (including cautions) are not covered by s.103(2). However, this has no practical effect because by the words in parenthesis in s.103(2), propensity can be established by wider means those provided by s.103(2).[221]

The exclusion in s.103(3) is limited to a propensity established via s.103(2).

Subsections 103(7) and (8) are parallel provisions for foreign convictions.

Under s.103(4)(a), offences are of the same description as each other if the statement of the offence in a written charge or indictment would, in each case, be in the same terms. This is fairly self-explanatory. In practice,

[219] *Tully and Wood* [2006] EWCA Crim 2270, [27]-[28].

[220] *Tully and Wood* [2006] EWCA Crim 2270, [27].

[221] E.g. *Valencia* [2015] EWCA Crim 857, [17].

it is largely made up of offences that fall under the same statutory provision.

Under s.103(4)(b), offences fall within the same category as each other if they are so specified in an order made by the Secretary of State. However, by s.103(5), any such category "*must consist of offences of the same type*" (as to which no definition is provided). This effectively limits the Secretary of State to compiling lists of offences that are of the same type; an order that seeks to group together offences that are not of the same type would presumably be unlawful. To date, only one such order has been made: the Criminal Justice Act 2003 (Categories of Offences) Order 2004/3346, which came into effect shortly after the bad character statutory provisions in 2004. The Order specifies a category of 11 theft-related offences, and a category of 36 sexual offences with a person under the age of 16. The Order is rarely relied upon, as in practice the required propensity is usually evident from the nature of the conviction and/or its particulars. Further, even if two offences appear in the same category, a propensity still has to be established to the court's satisfaction.

4.4.4 Important Matter In Issue

Per s.112(1), "'*important matter' means a matter of substantial importance in the context of the case as a whole*".

A deceptively simple phrase, the "*important matter in issue*" actually drives a large part of the operation of gateways (d) and (e), and thus is pivotal in the admission of the majority of bad character evidence that passes through s.101.

4.4.4.1 The Qualifier Of 'Importance'

The word "*important*" is used in gateways (d) and (e) (and also in gateway (c) but not in the context of "*matter in issue*").

In the context of "*matter in issue*" for gateways (d) and (e), 112(1) explains to an extent what "*important matter*" means.[222] The court is

[222] Section 112(1) does define "*important matter*" in terms identical to those used in s.100(1)(b)(ii), which is itself elaborated upon in s.100(3). This may be a remnant from

looking for *a matter of substantial importance in the context of the case as a whole where that matter is in issue between the defendant and prosecution, or between two co-defendants*. As a definition it is primarily self-defining. The legislation does not indicate what "*important*" or "*substantial importance*" means, or what "*matter*" means.

Given that it is part of the wording, however, "*important*" must be assumed to have some meaning. That meaning must go beyond mere relevance which is already a requirement in s.101(1)(d).[223] On a plain reading, "*important*" means that the issue must not be a peripheral or trivial one.

The requirement for importance is not often mentioned. Thus in *Anderson*, the only question the Court asked in this respect was whether the bad character evidence "*in this case [was] relevant to any issue between the prosecution and the defence?*"[224] There was no reference to importance. In *Purcell*, the Court said the bad character evidence was correctly admitted as "*relevant to the issues in the case*",[225] omitting any identification of an important matter. While in some of these cases it is merely the word that is missing, not the actual importance of the matter in issue, there are some cases where it might be said the matter in issue identified is not sufficiently important. One example is *Saint*.[226]

"*Important*" is also designed to keep the fact-finder's attention focused upon those matters that genuinely need to be decided in the case. For example, where bad character evidence is adduced not by way of conviction but by unproved allegations, the danger of distraction is even greater.

---

the draft Bill in which the same approach was to be adopted towards bad character evidence of both defendants and witnesses. On this reading, because s.112(1) uses "*important matter*" and s.100(1)(b) uses "*matter*" with the same definition for each term, the implication is that "*important*" adds nothing. It is also possible that the s.112 definition was meant to be informed by the factors in s.100(3). However, these may be unintended consequences of changes effected in the CJA.

223 See *Watters* [2007] EWCA Crim 1184, [18], citing *Archbold*.

224 *Anderson* [2008] EWCA Crim 837, [11].

225 *Purcell* [2007] EWCA Crim 2604, [25].

226 *Saint* [2010] EWCA Crim 1924, [20].

This has "*the dangers not only of adding to the length and cost of the trial, but of complicating the issues which the jury has to decide and taking the focus away from the most important issue or issues.*"[227]

Campbell emphasises "*importance*" in relation to the specific matter in issue in s.103(1)(b):

> *"The only circumstance in which there is likely to be an important issue as to whether a defendant has a propensity to tell lies is where telling lies is an element of the offence charged. Even then, the propensity to tell lies is only likely to be significant if the lying is in the context of committing criminal offences, in which case the evidence is likely to be admissible under s.103(1)(a)."*[228]

While *Campbell* adopts a restrictive interpretation as to credibility being an important matter in issue,[229] subsequent case law does establish that bad character will not automatically assist in determining truthfulness without something more. In particular, although the Court in *LH* states (perhaps a little unforgivingly) that "*[a]ny conviction for a criminal offence is likely to reflect on the credibility of the defendant*", it then goes on to say that "*[o]ld or isolated instances of untruthfulness are generally not likely to be of significant probative value on credibility.*" The fact that the Court focuses on instances of untruthfulness (as opposed to "*any conviction for a criminal offence*") suggests that *Campbell* is not far off the mark when it says that a defendant's credibility is only assisted by bad character where that bad character specifically shows a propensity to tell lies.[230]

---

227 *McKenzie* [2008] EWCA Crim 758, [23].

228 *Campbell* [2007] EWCA Crim 1472, [2007] 2 Cr App R 28, [31].

229 Thus in *LH* [2017] NICA 67, "*whether or not the defendant is being truthful is likely to be an important matter in issue between the defendant and the prosecution in many criminal trials.*"

230 Indeed the Court went on to say, "*We do not accept that a single incident where a defendant pleaded not guilty to an offence in respect of which he was subsequently convicted and gave an account which must have been rejected necessarily establishes a propensity for untruthfulness. In this case there were three other convictions in which the applicant had pleaded guilty. It was necessary to stand back and take those into account in determining*

Some guidance on "*substantial*" comes from the gateway (e) context in *Apabhai*, quoting from *Scott*: "*the word substantial must mean that the evidence concerned has something more than trivial probative value*".[231] Thus the court is looking for a significant, substantial, non-trivial matter in issue.

4.4.4.2 Matter In Issue

The CJA does not provide a definition of "*matter in issue*",[232] nor does it contrast it with 'fact in issue'.

A "*matter in issue*" can be framed at any level of abstraction. At the broadest level, the question 'whether the defendant is guilty' is a "*matter in issue*". So framed, it encompasses the myriad of different factual elements going to the question of guilt or innocence. Equally, the question whether the defendant has some kind of propensity might be a matter in issue. And at the narrow end of the spectrum is a specific factual dispute that needs resolving.

How the legislation intends the phrase to be used is unclear. It may be assumed that it was intended to be used as the Law Commission used it (although this does not necessarily aid clarity), but since there is no definition the phrase has tended to be used in whatever way seems appropriate in the context. In *Darnley* the Court used "*important matter in issue*" to mean: "*important evidence relating to an* issue in dispute *between the prosecution and the defence, within the meaning of gateway (d)*".[233] This

whether the propensity was established": *LH* [2017] NICA 67, [23]. See also *O'Sullivan* [2013] EWCA Crim 43,

[231] *Apabhai* [2011] EWCA Crim 917, [42] and *Scott* [2009] EWCA Crim 2457, [45].

[232] The phrase seems to have appeared first, in this context, in the Law Commission Report. It may have been adopted from the CLRC: *Evidence of Bad Character in Criminal Proceedings* (Law Com No 273, 2001), [11.8], quoting the CLRC Bill which uses the phrase. Although the Report refers to case law in sentences containing the phrase, it would appear that these cases have not actually employed that exact phrase. In the pre-CJA case of *Boardman v DPP* [1974] AC 421, their Lordships confine themselves to "*fact in question*": at 442.

[233] *Darnley* [2012] EWCA Crim 1148, [31] (emphasis added).

interpretation treats 'issue' as the thing in dispute, not 'matter' as the thing in *issue.*

The statutory guidance can be summarised as follows:

- From the two examples given (in s.103(1), and by implication in s.104(1)), a "*matter in issue*" can be a "*question whether the defendant has a propensity*" of two types. However, it is not limited to such a question.

- There are exceptions to the statutory assumption that a defendant's bad character is of probative value in determining guilt. This is what is meant by the concluding phrase of each of s.103(1)(a) and (b). The question whether the defendant has a propensity can have no probative value and can therefore be properly irrelevant (as opposed to being merely inadmissible).

Common matters in issue include:

- The elements of the offence charged, unless they are admitted by the defence.

- The defendant's propensity, either to commit offences of the kind charged or to be untruthful. These are created matters in issue by virtue of s.103(1) and s.104(1). Note that s.103(1)(b) is limited in application. The question of the defendant's propensity to be untruthful will normally only be capable of being described as an important matter in issue "*where telling lies is an element of the offence charged.*"[234]

- The "*genesis of the complaint*".[235]

---

[234] *Campbell* [2007] EWCA Crim 1472, [2007] 2 Cr App R 28, [15]. But note that *Highton* provides a way around this: see gateway (g) below.

[235] E.g. *M* [2009] EWCA Crim 2504, [10]. The circumstances in which C's allegations came to light were important; thus, the jury could be told that C made allegations when encouraged to do so by K, who also made similar allegations against D, although later withdrew them. The Court of Appeal did not object to that statement; it overruled the

- The defendant's state of mind[236] or intention.[237]

"*Matters in issue*" do not include:

- Facts which have been agreed by the parties.[238]

- Facts which do not assist the tribunal of fact to reach a verdict.[239]

Therefore, evidence that has (or may have) relevance only to these types of facts is inadmissible.

Matters in issue also do not include:

- Points that merely arise in the course of the investigation/trial and are not necessary for its resolution.

Problems commonly arise where (1) a peripheral matter is treated as an important matter, or where the matter is not actually in issue,[240] and (2)

---

decision to use gateway (d) only because the evidence was not of bad character within the meaning of s.112(1).

[236] *Brand* [2009] EWCA Crim 2878.

[237] *Swellings* [2009] EWCA Crim 3249, [2009] 2 Cr App R (S) 30: despite D's willingness to admit to manslaughter, there was still confusion about who had struck which blows. The defendant admitted he had struck one blow, but said he had then distanced himself from what followed. This meant that he did not accept he had been part of a joint enterprise after that point. Thus this physical act was still in dispute and so his propensity to street violence in a gang was relevant. The "*important matter in issue*" was this propensity.

[238] For example, the parties might agree that the complainant's watch was found in a pawn shop. The prosecution does not then need to prove that the watch found in the shop belongs to the complainant, and the defendant does not need to attempt to rebut it. Evidence that is relevant to that fact is therefore inadmissible for the purpose of proving that it is a true 'fact' or a false 'fact'.

[239] For example, if the defendant is charged with an offence of strict liability, his assertion that he did not intend to commit the act would not affect the verdict (although it may affect sentence).

[240] E.g. in *Mustapha* [2007] EWCA Crim 1702, [13], the judge said the "*important question*" (not important matter in issue) was whether the defendant had a propensity to possess firearms and live ammunition. The Court of Appeal agreed that this was an

where inadequate reasoning is given for the identification of a matter in issue.

See *Saint*, discussed in the context of gateway (c) above. The defendant was convicted (in 2009) of false imprisonment, two indecent assaults, and rape against C, occurring in a car park in 1989. The judge had wrongly admitted bad character evidence via gateway (c) to the effect that in the mid-1990s the defendant visited the car park at night.

In respect of gateway (d), propensity could not be the matter in issue, but there was another possibility because "*the Crown had a legitimate interest in proving that the appellant was in the habit of frequenting the car park and the surrounding area late at night.*"[241] However, as the Court said, this is only an *interest*, not a matter in issue: the case could be proved without showing the habit. In fact, evidence showing that the defendant simply had this habit is by itself not even bad character evidence, although in this case there were bad character aspects as well, mainly those that alleged non-consensually watching other people having sexual intercourse.

The prosecution also suggested that the evidence could help to establish the identity of the person whose footsteps had been heard prior to the assault. The prosecution was better able to prove that identity if it could adduce evidence not just of the defendant's habit of frequenting the area late at night but also of his interest in watching people having sex.[242] The Court of Appeal said this was unlikely to constitute an important matter in issue. "*[R]ealistically and in the light of all the other evidence in the case, the footsteps issue was probably not of 'substantial importance' and did not justify the admission of the bad character evidence under gateway (d).*"[243]

---

incorrect use of s.103(1)(a), because the present offence was not about firearm possession.

241 *Saint* [2010] EWCA Crim 1924, [19].

242 The footsteps were heard just after the complainant had had consensual sexual intercourse in her car with another man.

243 *Saint* [2010] EWCA Crim 1924, [20]. It was not relevant that the defendant was also involved in consensual promiscuity at the time: at [19]. This would be to mistake prejudice for relevance.

The evidence having been wrongly admitted under both gateways (c) and (d), the conviction was unsafe.

Evidence associating a person with a gang can be gateway (d) evidence. In *Lewis* the Court of Appeal confirmed that evidence that D was a member of, or associated with, street/criminal gangs in a relevant area was admissible under gateway (d):

> *"Analysing the issue in a case such as the present, there are four questions that a judge has to consider:*
>
> *(1) Is the evidence relevant to an important matter in issue between a defendant and the prosecution?*
>
> *(2) Is there proper evidence of the existence and nature of the gang or gangs?*
>
> *(3) Does the evidence, if accepted, go to show the defendant was a member of or associated with a gang or gangs which exhibited violence or hostility to the police or with links with firearms?*
>
> *(4) If the evidence is admitted, will it have such an adverse effect on the fairness of the proceedings that it ought to be excluded?"*[244]

Proper evidence for the purposes of question (2) can include expert police evidence based on accumulated knowledge and experience. In *Rashid*, five categories of evidence (including a police officer's expert evidence) as to the membership and activities of gangs in a particular area, and the meaning of language said to be used by them, were rightly admitted as bad character evidence. In fact, this evidence was treated as both s.98(a) and gateway (d) evidence, capable of showing that the defendants were "*members or associated with gangs which exhibited violence or hostility and links with firearms*".[245]

In *Okokono*, discussed above in relation to gateway (c), one of the three ways in which bad character evidence was said to be admissible was under

[244] *Lewis* [2014] EWCA Crim 48, [2014] 2 Cr App R (S) 27, [82].

[245] *Rashid* [2019] EWCA Crim 2018, [36]-[37].

gateway (d): to establish D's willingness to engage in gang fights, knowing that others had a propensity to use knives to lethal effect.[246] One difficulty with this reasoning is that D's conviction was only for possession of a knife. There was no evidence that he had engaged in a fight at the time of that conviction.

In another gang-related case, *Mullings*, the defendant was convicted of possessing a firearm with intent to endanger life. He and several other defendants were said to be part of a gang that had confronted a rival gang. The subsequent events led to a murder. The defendant did not himself carry a firearm. The question was whether he was aware that others in the group were carrying firearms with the requisite intent, and participated with that knowledge and with the same intention.[247] He was arrested in March 2007; in November 2007 letters sent to him in prison were found. They included material about the particular gangs, showing allegiances and enmities held by the unknown authors.

The Court of Appeal held that the defendant's receipt and/or retention of the letters[248] could be used by the jury as evidence of bad character which went to the question whether the appellant participated in a group activity of whose objectives he was aware.[249] It did not matter that the letters were received after the event, or that he had not himself expressed the views contained within the letters. It was admissible under gateway (d) since it went to an important issue in the case.[250] If it was not bad character evidence, it was admissible under the common law as relevant to the issues of joint possession and intention.

---

[246] *Okokono* [2014] EWCA Crim 2521, [60]. See also *Awoyemi* [2016] EWCA Crim 668; *Stewart* [2016] EWCA Crim 447; *Lunkulu* [2015] EWCA Crim 1350.

[247] *Mullings* [2010] EWCA Crim 2820, [2011] 2 Cr App R 2, [10].

[248] *Mullings* [2010] EWCA Crim 2820, [2011] 2 Cr App R 2, [22]: "*the possession and retention of these documents constituted evidence from which the jury could infer that the appellant identified himself with the sentiments they expressed. Had the letters been admitted to prove a disposition towards misconduct the jury would have required a careful direction to the effect that they could not use the letters for this purpose unless they were sure that possession and/or retention of the letters established the appellant's disposition.*"

[249] *Mullings* [2010] EWCA Crim 2820, [2011] 2 Cr App R 2, [32].

[250] With neither s.78 of PACE nor s.101(3) operating on the facts.

It may be asked how letters written by another can be relevant to the defendant's "*disposition*". There are many reasons why he might receive or retain the letters, not necessarily casting light on his own disposition or indicating reprehensible behaviour. The only real relevance is that the defendant's knowledge (now evidenced in the letters) of the behaviour of known gang members may have informed his presence and intention at the scene of the crime earlier in the year. Whether this is true bad character evidence might be open to debate.

The cases on gang-membership and association are not always easy to reconcile with the law on guilt by association. In *Hassan*, a murder trial, largely uncharged/non-conviction evidence of D's association with drugs and drug dealers was admissible under gateway (d) as going to the motive for the killing.[251] *Hassan* distinguished *Kane*, which strongly criticised the use of evidence to show "*guilt by association*". In *Kane*, D's close involvement or association with others having extensive criminal convictions was inadmissible at his trial for blackmail:

> *"The propensity is not to be equated with some kind of propensity to commit offences generally. [The prosecution] has been more or less explicit in saying that really why the prosecution wanted this evidence in was that they indeed wanted the jury to know 'the nature of the man with whom they were dealing.' That cannot possibly in itself be a sufficient justification for admitting the evidence or a sufficient justification for the prosecution even to try and persuade the Crown Court judge to admit that evidence. Guilt by association of itself has never been part of England and Wales criminal law."*[252]

In *Urushadze* the question was whether D was part of a joint enterprise to rob the victim, or whether he had not witnessed the first part of the incident and was only trying to defend an acquaintance against people apparently attacking him. D had previous convictions for shoplifting which were admitted under gateway (d). It was said that the convictions were relevant to the matter in issue of the defendant's propensity "*to know*

[251] *Hassan* [2020] EWCA Crim 761, [15].

[252] *Kane* [2013] EWCA Crim 1487, [29]-[30].

and perceive that a theft was taking place—a theft with violence, hence a robbery".[253]

The Court of Appeal said the evidence should not have been admitted under any circumstances, because the propensity to know that a theft is taking place (if such a thing exists) was not capable of being established by the convictions. Moreover, the present charge was for violent theft whereas the convictions were for shoplifting, unlikely to cast any light on how the defendant perceived the present events or to establish a propensity to commit robbery of the type in question. Even if it did have limited probative value, this was "*very greatly outweighed*" by the prejudice caused; s.101(3) should have been applied.[254]

In *Bello*, D was accused of fraudulently passing on customers' credit cards to a co-defendant. The bad character evidence suggested that D had, six months earlier fraudulently used a customer's credit card to transfer money to a friend's credit card. In D's home was a piece of paper containing a credit card number and expiry date. They matched those of a credit card that had been issued to the defendant's friend, allegedly fraudulently, in the uncharged set of events. The judge had no doubt as to the relevance of the piece of paper: "*I have no doubt … that this evidence was relevant under section 101(1)(d) … It is, in my judgment, plainly relevant to an important matter in issue between the defendant and the prosecution, which is* whether the defendant has committed this offence."[255]

This approach widens the "*matter in issue*" as far as it can possibly go, making the 'matter' equivalent to the defendant's 'guilt'. This approach illustrates the opposite extreme to the 'peripheral matters problem' raised above. It holds that "*an important matter in issue*" can be applied so broadly as to encompass the actual question of the defendant's guilt—which is the preoccupation of any trial on a plea of not guilty. It does not need to be a specific matter.

---

253 *Urushadze* [2008] EWCA Crim 2498, [21].

254 *Urushadze* [2008] EWCA Crim 2498, [28].

255 *Bello* [2007] EWCA Crim 2499, [8] (emphasis added).

Caution is needed to avoid the eventuality *Hanson* warned against in the context of gateway (d): the prosecution making routine applications to admit bad character evidence without regard to the circumstances of each case.[256]

4.5 Gateway (e): S.101(1)(e)

"(e) it has substantial probative value in relation to an important matter in issue between the defendant and a co-defendant"

"104 'Matter in issue between the defendant and a co-defendant'

(1) Evidence which is relevant to the question whether the defendant has a propensity to be untruthful is admissible on that basis under section 101(1)(e) only if the nature or conduct of his defence is such as to undermine the co-defendant's defence.

(2) Only evidence—

> *(a) which is to be (or has been) adduced by the co-defendant, or*
>
> *(b) which a witness is to be invited to give (or has given) in cross-examination by the co-defendant,*

is admissible under section 101(1)(e)."

4.5.1 What Is A Co-Defendant?

Section 112(1) provides the following definitions:

"'defendant', in relation to criminal proceedings, means a person charged with an offence in those proceedings;

"'co- defendant', in relation to a defendant, means a person charged with an offence in the same proceedings."

256 *Hanson* [2005] EWCA Crim 824, [2005] 2 Cr App R 21, [4].

For most practical purposes, this means a person who is charged on the same indictment as D1.

However, a person who was originally a co-defendant (D2) but has, before trial, been dealt with another way (e.g. entered an acceptable plea and awaits sentence pending the conclusion of D1's trial on the same or related charges) is *not* a co-defendant for the purposes of D1's trial.[257] Thus, an application to adduce evidence of D2's bad character must be made under s.100, not gateway (e).

If D2 is tried in his absence, he is still a co-defendant and gateway (e) can be used. Of course, D2's absence is likely to mean that there are fewer matters in issue available for D1 to use.[258]

4.5.2 Substantial Probative Value

In theory, this phrase bears the same meaning as in s.100(1)(b).

However, in the context of gateway (e), it bears particular importance (see Chapter 5 on exclusions).

In *Phillips* it was held that, in order to satisfy gateway (e), "*where the defendant is seeking to prove a relevant propensity he must first establish that … the evidence is substantially probative of the propensity* and *that the propensity alleged is substantially probative of the fact in issue.*"[259]

It is correct that evidence of the defendant's bad character must be substantially probative of the important matter in issue (commonly, propensity to commit similar offences or untruthfulness). But the legislation does not require that the propensity be "*substantially probative*" of any 'fact in issue'. It merely needs to be of substantial *importance* in the

---

[257] *Jukes* [2018] EWCA Crim 176.

[258] *Lee* [2005] EWCA Crim 3459: "*Had [D2] been present to assert more than he had [in a previous interview], a sufficiently important issue might have arisen to have resulted in [D1's] convictions going before the jury, but given [D2's] absence that would not be possible*" at [17].

[259] *Phillips* [2011] EWCA Crim 2935, [2012] 1 Cr App R 25, [41] (emphasis in original).

context of the case as a whole. The propensity itself is the matter in issue, and does not, under the bad character provisions, have to have relevance to any other issue in the case (whether "*matter in issue*" or 'fact in issue'), although of course it may do so.

What is clear from *Phillips* is the reformulation of the meaning of "*substantial probative value*" in the special context of gateway (e).

The Court of Appeal rejected the old meaning of "*something more than trivial probative value*", replacing it with the concept of "*an enhanced capability of proving or disproving a matter in issue*".[260] This also applies to the test under s.100(1)(b).[261] It is clear that one effect of this higher standard of admission is to make it harder for a defendant to use another's bad character, under both gateway (e) (in respect of a co-defendant), and s.100(1)(b) (in respect of a prosecution witness).

In case law applying *Phillips*[262] a further embellishment has emerged, that the enhanced relevance meaning of "*substantial probative value*" in s.100(1)(b) (and, presumably therefore, s.101(1)(e)) also requires accounting for the threat of satellite litigation. In *Dizaei* the Court of Appeal said, citing *Phillips*, that

> *"If … the judge correctly directs the jury that they must not consider the alleged bad character evidence unless they are sure that it is true, two trials would be simultaneously in progress before the same jury. …*
>
> *"In our judgment these are relevant considerations bearing on the assessment of the probative value of the evidence sought to be adduced and its importance in the overall context of the*

---

[260] *Phillips* [2011] EWCA Crim 2935, [2012] 1 Cr App R 25, [39]. This is a higher test than that of "*marginal or trivial value*" in the Explanatory Notes to the CJA, [375].

[261] "*[T]he legal meaning of the term 'substantial probative value' must be the same*" for both gateway (e) and s.100(1)(b): *Phillips* [2011] EWCA Crim 2935, [2012] 1 Cr App R 25, [38].

[262] *Turnbull* [2013] EWCA Crim 676 (gateway (e)); *Walsh* [2012] EWCA Crim 2728; *Sixto* [2012] EWCA Crim 2615; *Dizaei* [2013] EWCA Crim 88, [2013] 1 Cr App R 31.

> *case. When it is assessing the probative value of the evidence in accordance with s.100(1)(b) and s.100(3), and consistently with s.100(2), among the factors relevant to the admissibility judgment, the court should reflect whether the admission of the evidence relating to the bad character of the witness might make it difficult for the jury to understand the remainder of the evidence, and whether its understanding of the case as a whole might be diminished. In such cases the conclusion may be that the evidence is not of substantial probative value … or that the evidence is not of substantial importance in the context of the case as a whole, or both. If so, the pre-conditions to admissibility will not established."*[263]

Thus, the assessment of substantial probative value of bad character evidence now includes the risk that the jury might become distracted from its focus on the offence at hand by the admission of that evidence. *Dizaei* treats this as a factor that may be considered under s.100(3), which is allowed by the non-closed nature of the list therein. It is, however, somewhat different to the factors that are listed in s.100(3), which concern the value of the bad character evidence itself, upon the assumption (s.109) that it is true. The focus is not upon proving that the evidence is true, which is the cause of the problem of satellite litigation. It might be argued that such a factor is not relevant[264] to the assessment of probative value.

However, as discussed in Chapter 5 (exclusions), this approach to "*substantial probative value*" is designed partly to counter the lack of any exclusionary provision in respect of gateway (e). Where prosecution evidence is concerned and an exclusionary provision exists (such as s.101(3) or s.78), the risk of satellite litigation falls to be considered when exercising that exclusionary power, not when deciding admissibility under a relevance-based test. The *Phillips* line of reasoning has, in an effort

---

[263] *Dizaei* [2013] EWCA Crim 88, [2013] 1 Cr App R 31, [37]-[38]. Note that s.100(1)(b)(ii) does not actually lead to a conclusion "*that the evidence is not of substantial importance in the context of the case as a whole*". s.100(1)(b)(ii) relates to the "*matter*", not the "*evidence*".

[264] Section 100(3) begins: "*In assessing the probative value of evidence for the purposes of subsection (1)(b) the court must have regard to the following factors (and to any others it considers* relevant*)* …" (emphasis added).

to provide a substitute-exclusionary power, included such considerations in the test for substantial probative value for defence evidence.[265]

What is the difference between "*relevance*" and "*substantial probative value*"?

Prima facie, relevance is a lower threshold than substantial probative value.

This can be illustrated by the case of *McLean* (*Edwards and Rowlands*), where bad character evidence was inadmissible via gateway (d) but admissible via gateway (e).

D1 was convicted of two counts of wounding with intent. He had previous convictions for wounding with intent using a knife in 1998, two offences of battery in 2001, and affray in 2004.

The prosecution's 'application' to admit these via gateway (d), to establish a propensity for violence, was rejected.[266]

However, the judge then admitted the convictions at the behest of D2 under gateway (e). The judge ruled that the important matter in issue between the defendants was created by the separate versions of events that were put forward by each defendant, and that D1's bad character had substantial probative value in relation to that issue. "*[I]f each defendant was saying he was not involved in the violence, and one has previous convictions for violence, that must have substantial probative value on the issue between them.*"[267] It could be said that this looks very similar to the prosecution's propensity argument: if a defendant has convictions for violent

[265] Given its focus on the lack of exclusionary provisions for defence evidence, the Court in *Phillips* probably did not intend to suggest modifications to the existing exclusionary provisions for prosecution evidence.

[266] *Edwards and Rowlands* [2005] EWCA Crim 3244, [2006] 2 Cr App R 4, [48].

[267] *Edwards and Rowlands* [2005] EWCA Crim 3244, [2006] 2 Cr App R 4, [51].

behaviour, this may influence the question whether he has committed the present offence involving violent behaviour.[268]

D1 challenged this decision, asking why the gateway (e) application succeeded but the application to pass the less stringent relevance threshold in gateway (d) had failed.

The Court of Appeal said that "*[d]ifferent considerations applied to the co-defendant's application which was made under a different provision, namely s.101(1)(e).*"[269] However, it is also true that there are many *similar* considerations between the two gateways. In particular, the essence of the "*matter in issue*" in both gateway (d) and gateway (e) was based upon the fact that both D1's convictions and the present charge involved violence.

When two gateways have been applied in respect of the same evidence with different outcomes, it should be possible to confirm correct application of the law by identifying which elements of the second gateway have given the different result.

This is especially so when gateways (d) and (e) are concerned, because they are very similar.

- Their points of difference are
    - "*Substantial probative value*" rather than "*relevant*";
    - The parties between whom the matter in issue arises.[270]
- The points of similarity are
    - The requirement for a "*matter in issue*";

---

[268] For a case where there was no real difference, see *Khan* [2015] EWCA Crim 1755, [11]-[16].

[269] *Edwards and Rowlands* [2005] EWCA Crim 3244, [2006] 2 Cr App R 4, [49].

[270] There is also the qualification in s.104(1), which was not applicable in this case, and the exclusions to gateway (d), which were not applied and, if they were, would only apply after the assessment of the elements of the gateway.

- o The requirement that it be important;
- o The base requirement of "*relevant*" (because the higher standard in gateway (e) must necessarily satisfy this lower common standard).

Where one piece of evidence is tested against both gateways, then, it is possible to identify (1) whether each gateway concerns the same matter in issue in respect of which the evidence is said to be relevant, (2) whether the matter is important in both gateways as between the respective parties, and (3) whether the evidence is relevant in respect of both gateways.

4.5.3 Matter In Issue Between Defendants

Examples of matters in issue:

- See above possible "*matters in issue*" in relation to gateway (d). These include common matters in issue such as propensity to commit particular kinds of offences or to behave in a particular way.
- Section 104(1) creates an additional matter in issue: propensity to be untruthful is a matter in issue if the nature or conduct of D1's defence is such as to undermine D2's defence. This is narrower than s.103(1)(b). The purpose of showing D1's propensity to be untruthful is usually to influence the jury's belief in his defence, that is, whether or not he committed the offence.[271] However, s.104(1) is just one example of a matter in issue. It is not mandatory in all gateway (e) cases.[272]
- A matter in issue between co-defendants can be created or triggered by prosecution actions or tactics.

[271] *De Vos* [2006] EWCA Crim 1688, [17].

[272] *Daly* [2014] EWCA Crim 2117, [14]-[15].

- A matter in issue between a defendant and the prosecution can also be a matter in issue between co-defendants.
- The credibility of a defendant is a matter in issue for gateway (e) purposes.[273]

In *West*, D was convicted of murder and false imprisonment. His co-defendants, O and B, were both acquitted. D had convictions for dishonesty, and O had numerous convictions, including four counts of actual bodily harm, two s.20 wounding offences, affray, and an assault on the police. There had been no indication of any cut-throat defences. After D gave evidence, and before O was to give evidence, D indicated that he wished to cross-examine O about his previous convictions. The judge refused, on the basis that it would not be possible to ensure fair trial for O, especially as D had already given evidence.[274] However, when the prosecution cross-examined O, O blamed D for the killing, stating that D had "*whacked*" the victim. D again applied to cross-examine O about O's previous convictions.[275] The judge refused, this time because the "*matter in issue was not an issue between [the defendant] and [O] but an issue between [O] and the prosecution*".[276]

Plainly, as the Court of Appeal held, there was undoubtedly an important matter in issue for gateway (e) purposes,[277] even though the situation had been created by an interaction between the prosecution and a co-defendant. O's convictions, and particularly those for violent offences, went to

[273] See *Rosato* [2008] EWCA Crim 1243, [22]: "*In this case there is no dispute that there was an important matter in issue between the appellant and [D2], because the effect of the appellant's evidence was to put the responsibility for the arson onto the shoulders of [D2]. [D2] therefore had an interest in being able to deploy before the jury any material properly relevant in considering whether they should regard this appellant as a credible witness.*"

[274] *West* [2006] EWCA Crim 1843, [17].

[275] Of course, not only is this not an 'application', but in gateway (e) cases the judge has only a very limited discretion if all conditions are satisfied.

[276] *West* [2006] EWCA Crim 1843, [19].

[277] *West* [2006] EWCA Crim 1843, [21].

a matter in issue between the defendants, namely who was telling the truth about the violence suffered by the victim.

In a case like *West*, carefully identifying the matter in issue may make it easier to identify which parties might be affected by it.[278]

Obeng sets out the approach where defendants are not facing a joint charge *and* there is no cut-throat defence:

- *"first, what is the fact in issue*[279] *between the defendants;*
- *secondly, is that an important issue between them;*
- *thirdly, does the antecedent character have substantial probative value in resolving that issue; and,*
- *fourthly, does the resolution of that issue assist with the ultimate issue?"*[280]

A matter in issue does not necessarily arise just because defendants give different versions of what happened. *Edwards and Rowlands* states that a mere denial of participation may not give rise to a matter in issue that satisfies gateway (e).[281] Whether it is a mere denial will be a question of fact.[282]

A matter in issue between co-defendants does not arise if it is only in issue between one defendant and the prosecution. Thus in *Woolley* the judge

---

[278] In *McAfee* [2006] EWCA Crim 2914 the matter in issue might have been credibility, propensity to commit arson, or whether the defendant had been taking drugs. Given that four gateways were being discussed ((d), (e), (f) and (g)), it may have assisted to identify distinctly the matter in issue for each of (d) and (e). The failure to do so is complicated by the fact that the co-defendant, not the prosecution, made the specific arguments about gateways (f) and (g).

[279] Presumably meaning "*matter in issue*".

[280] *Obeng* [2016] EWCA Crim 1797, [32].

[281] *Edwards and Rowlands* [2005] EWCA Crim 3244, [2006] 2 Cr App R 4, [1](vi).

[282] See *Edwards and Rowlands* [2005] EWCA Crim 3244, [2006] 2 Cr App R 4, [25] where the Court held that Rowlands made more than a mere denial. Also, the case of *McLean* where simply giving "*separate versions of what had occurred*" created an "*important issue*" between the defendants: [51].

was correct to hold that evidence which "*might prove that [D1] was more involved in the production and supply of cannabis ... did not prove that [D2] was not, or was less likely to be, involved, which was the real issue as between [D2] and [D1].*"[283] The matter to which the bad character evidence was relevant was D1's propensity to engage in drug-related offences, which went to his own guilt. That was a matter for the prosecution. On these particular facts, D1's tendency to engage in drug-related offences did not indicate D2's innocence.

4.6 Gateway (f): S.101(1)(f)

"(f) it is evidence to correct a false impression given by the defendant"

"105 'Evidence to correct a false impression'

(1) For the purposes of section 101(1)(f)—

(a) the defendant gives a false impression if he is responsible for the making of an express or implied assertion which is apt to give the court or jury a false or misleading impression about the defendant;

(b) evidence to correct such an impression is evidence which has probative value in correcting it.

(2) A defendant is treated as being responsible for the making of an assertion if—

(a) the assertion is made by the defendant in the proceedings (whether or not in evidence given by him),

(b) the assertion was made by the defendant—

(i) on being questioned under caution, before charge, about the offence with which he is charged, or

283 *Woolley* [2011] EWCA Crim 2758, [15].

(ii) on being charged with the offence or officially informed that he might be prosecuted for it, and evidence of the assertion is given in the proceedings,

(c) the assertion is made by a witness called by the defendant,

(d) the assertion is made by any witness in cross-examination in response to a question asked by the defendant that is intended to elicit it, or is likely to do so, or

(e) the assertion was made by any person out of court, and the defendant adduces evidence of it in the proceedings.

(3) A defendant who would otherwise be treated as responsible for the making of an assertion shall not be so treated if, or to the extent that, he withdraws it or disassociates himself from it.

(4) Where it appears to the court that a defendant, by means of his conduct (other than the giving of evidence) in the proceedings, is seeking to give the court or jury an impression about himself that is false or misleading, the court may if it appears just to do so treat the defendant as being responsible for the making of an assertion which is apt to give that impression.

(5) In subsection (4) 'conduct' includes appearance or dress.

(6) Evidence is admissible under section 101(1)(f) only if it goes no further than is necessary to correct the false impression.

(7) Only prosecution evidence is admissible under section 101(1)(f)."

Gateway (f) is not very commonly employed, nor does it attract a great deal of analysis in the courts. This may be attributed to its comparatively specific threshold requirement which, unlike gateways (c) or (d), cannot readily be expanded to cover a number of associated scenarios.[284] It is quite frequently rejected for failing to apply on the facts.

A defendant must give a false impression about himself, either by express or implied assertion, following which the prosecution may adduce evidence of his bad character only to correct that impression.

4.6.1 When Is An Impression False?

The legislation does not set out how the judge decides whether a false impression has actually been given.[285] In many cases, the judge will need to consider if there is sufficient evidence that shows a false impression has been given (such evidence does not necessarily then go before the jury).

A distinction is drawn between bad character evidence being admitted to correct a false impression, which is subject to s.105(1)(b) and s.109,[286] and the basis upon which the judge finds that the defendant has given a false impression, thus opening the gateway for the admission of the bad character evidence.

Sometimes the two are the same, as, for example, where the defendant asserts that he has never been in trouble with the police, but there are records indicating that he has been cautioned for an offence. In this example, neither the existence of a false impression nor the evidence being used to correct it is in dispute.

---

[284] The Court of Appeal is also rather swift to address such misuses: see, e.g. *Eyidah* [2010] EWCA Crim 987, where no false impression had been identified at all. However contrast *Lewis* [2008] EWCA Crim 424, where it was arguable whether D was giving a false impression about himself; and in any event a co-defendant cannot use gateway (f).

[285] The Explanatory Notes to the CJA, [376] only contemplate the situation where there is no doubt that what the defendant has said is not actually the case: "*This might be done expressly, for example, by claiming to be of good character when this is not the case, or implied, for example, by leading evidence of his conduct that carries an implication that he is of a better character than is actually the case.*"

[286] Section 105(1)(b) requires that bad character evidence must have probative value in correcting the false impression, and s.109 requires the court to assume that the evidence is true for the purpose of determining admissibility.

The problem arises when the prosecution suggests there has been a false impression based on some evidence that is itself disputed.

There is no false impression when merely contradicting prosecution case. A classic case is where the prosecution says that the defendant is giving a false impression because certain prosecution evidence already being used in the case suggests that he is. Plainly, this would be unfair:

> *"The only basis on which it could be said that he was a drug dealer, (in the face of denials of that fact ...) was by the very evidence that the Crown wished to adduce, viz. the texts. There was no other evidence to suggest it and it was not a positive case being put by the Crown. The appellant had admitted he was a Class A drug user and he had admitted his past convictions. We therefore cannot see the basis on which the section 101(1)(f) 'gateway' could have been properly invoked."*[287]

Is an impression "*false*" because it is inconsistent with other allegations?

Giving the impression that one is not the sort of person to commit the present crime might be sufficient to constitute a false impression. Care should be taken not to distract the jury with satellite litigation by asking them to decide whether other, similar, allegations are true, in order to then use them to correct an alleged false impression.[288]

This situation arose in *Weir*, where a priest was charged with rape of a female member of his temple. He gave the impression in interview, and via character witnesses, that he had never behaved inappropriately towards female worshippers. The bad character evidence came from two other women (possibly from a different temple) who alleged the defendant made sexually-charged approaches to them. The Court of Appeal said:

---

[287] *Chrysostomou* [2010] EWCA Crim 1403, [37].

[288] This also risks trying to establish propensity by coincidence evidence: see Chapter 6 on cross-admissibility.

> *"In our judgment the evidence of the two women was admissible under section 101(1)(f) because part of the false impression given by the appellant in interview and, as it turned out later by calling seven character witnesses, was that he was a priest who had never behaved inappropriately towards female worshippers at his temple."*[289]

However, the defendant had also denied any inappropriate behaviour towards these two women. *Weir* allows disputed allegations to be used to rebut the giving of an assertion that is only false if the allegations are believed.[290]

Giving an impression of general good character can trigger gateway (f).

Recently, in *Cleere*, the Court held that a misleading impression had been given when D1 emphasised "*the positive aspects of [his] character in caring for [a family member] in a devoted manner.*" However, the "*way in which the evidence came out, which was effectively on the spur of the moment in response to cross-examination by a co-defendant's counsel*", meant that the Court would not have admitted the bad character evidence.[291]

In *Jalil* the defendant was convicted of conspiracy to murder, in a terrorism-related conspiracy. In chief he stated that he was a businessman working in the mobile telephone industry, and had told this to the police. In cross-examination on his behalf it was asserted that the police had found a business plan for his company while searching his home. The implication was that he was an honest businessman and that the police investigation supported this. Evidence was then admitted under gateway (f) suggesting that the defendant's company was actually being used for fraudulent purposes, possibly carousel or missing trader fraud, unrelated to the alleged terrorist activity.

---

289 *Weir* [2005] EWCA Crim 2866, [2006] 1 Cr App R 19, [43].

290 A similar situation arose in *S* [2007] EWCA Crim 1387, [17]: "*the result of admitting the evidence in question resulted in a very substantial proportion of the trial being taken up in what might be called a 'collateral' issue relating to the previous behaviour of the appellant; and that type of situation is clearly one which should be avoided if possible so that the issues in the trial do not become distorted.*"

291 *Cleere* [2020] EWCA Crim 1360, [18]-[19].

> *"The judge was entitled to say that the jury would be left with a misleading impression, as a result of the defendant's evidence, if it carried away the message that he was a bona fide businessman and for that reason less likely to be guilty of association with terrorist endeavour."*[292]

See also *Amponsah,* where the defendant was charged with fraudulent evasion of the prohibition on the importation of cocaine, and had a conviction for theft in 1996. The Court said:

> *"The impression being given was that of a hard-working, truthful, church-going individual and the evidence was properly balanced by the consideration of the fact that notwithstanding this impression she sought to convey, she had in fact been convicted of an offence of dishonesty."*[293]

Does putting forward a defence constitute giving a false impression?

The defendant does not give a false impression merely by asserting that he has not committed the crime at all. In *Iqbal,* the alleged false impression was the defendant's explanation for why his DNA was on a heroin package. The Court of Appeal held that this was not a false impression:

> *"Even if what is contained in a defence case statement can amount to an assertion made by a defendant in the proceedings, the document in reality is setting out the contentions of the defence in relation to a fundamental issue in the case, the nature of his defence and the matters of fact upon which he takes issue. This, in the court's judgment, is not an impression about him, let alone a false or misleading one without begging the very question which the jury would have to determine."*[294]

However, there are some cases where it is not so clear that the defendant is merely presenting his defence. In *H,* the defendant was convicted of

---

[292] *Jalil* [2008] EWCA Crim 2910, [49]. Arguably, gateway (f) might have worked in this way in *Haigh* [2010] EWCA Crim 90.

[293] *Amponsah* [2005] EWCA Crim 2993.

[294] *Iqbal* [2006] EWCA Crim 1302, [16].

five counts of rape of a child and three counts of attempted rape of a child (specimen counts), against the seven/eight-year old daughter of his partner.[295] He had numerous previous convictions, including one of a sexual nature bearing strong similarities to an allegation of oral rape at knifepoint made by the complainant. The judge admitted all convictions via gateways (d) and (f). The latter gateway was applicable because, in police interviews, the defendant was asked about the allegation that he had held a knife to the complainant's throat at the time he was orally raping her. He said, "*I would not do that*". A little later he said, "*I don't punish her by sticking my dick in her face. That is not the type of person I am*". The prosecution argument was that these statements gave a false impression because it was demonstrable that the defendant had done exactly these things in the past, albeit to someone else.

What is not made clear is whether the knifepoint rape was one of the specimen counts, or part of the general background of events being related by complainant. If it was one of the specimen counts, then it is arguable that the defendant was merely presenting his defence, i.e. that he did not rape the complainant and, perhaps, would not do such things to her in particular. If so, it would not constitute a false impression. On the other hand, if it was not a specimen count, then the complainant's account of the knifepoint rape should not have been allowed in evidence without a separate bad character evidence application. We then face the problem that if the defendant denies an event said to be a part of bad character evidence, can that denial be considered the giving of a false impression and thus the gateway for more bad character evidence? This presents a potentially interminable spiral of bad character evidence.

4.6.2 Making, And Withdrawing From, A False Impression

4.6.2.1 Making a false impression

The false impression must be given by the defendant, or be given at his instigation. While this would seem to cover statements made by the defendant, the Court has suggested, *obiter*, that there might be an exception where the defendant gives an answer to a direct question in police

[295] *H* [2006] EWCA Crim 2898.

interview.[296] Perhaps the false impression is not "*given by the defendant*" if it is in response to a leading question by police and is not something the defendant intended to be part of his case at trial.

In *Cleere*, the "*way in which the evidence came out, which was effectively on the spur of the moment in response to cross-examination by a co-defendant's counsel*" was one factor in the Court's decision that the bad character evidence should not have been admitted.[297]

By s.105(4) and (5), much of the old law dealing with when a defendant makes a statement, including by his clothing or conduct, has been adopted post-CJA. Thus:

- The wearing of a particular clothing, e.g. religious garb or regimental blazer.[298]

- Having an "*extravagant lifestyle*"[299] or possessing large sums of money[300] might be the subject of a false impression if the defendant gives an explanation for them that can be rebutted by bad character evidence, usually in the form of allegations that the defendant engages in criminal activities that produce money.

However, such cases do tend to risk excessive satellite litigation as well as overlap with disputed evidence that is already part of the prosecution's case against the defendant. The case law has not tended formally to identify these issues as gateway (f) issues.

The gateway is not activated if a defendant gives a false impression about someone or something other than the defendant: s.105(1)(a).

The impression must be *about* the defendant himself, not merely *made by* the defendant. In *Hanson* the judge rejected gateway (f), because the

---

296 *RB* [2008] EWCA Crim 1850, [35]. See also *Good* [2008] EWCA Crim 2923.

297 *Cleere* [2020] EWCA Crim 1360, [18]-[19].

298 *Saleem* [2007] EWCA Crim 1923, [22].

299 *Green* [2009] EWCA Crim 1688.

300 *Graham* [2007] EWCA Crim 1499.

defendant's assertion (that the complainant had a motive to have the defendant removed from the matrimonial home) was not *about the defendant.*[301]

There is a distinction between the defendant making a merely inconsistent statement, or even telling a lie, and the giving of a false impression about himself.

In *Lovelock* there was no false impression about the defendant: he was merely (perhaps unwisely) giving two different reasons for secreting money in another country. He made one statement at trial, and another in an earlier statement. The previous statement he had made about the money could have been adduced to show that he had given a different explanation, and thus to cast doubt on the credibility of his defence. There was no need to treat the second statement in court as a false impression in order to do this.[302]

4.6.2.2 Withdrawing from a false impression

Just as the defendant must be responsible for the making of the false impression, he can also decide to withdraw from it.

Section 105(3) explicitly provides that the defendant will not be treated as being responsible for making an assertion if he "*withdraws or disassociates himself from it.*"

---

[301] *Hanson* [2005] EWCA Crim 824, [2005] 2 Cr App R 21, [51]. See also *Jarvis* [2008] EWCA Crim 488.

[302] *Lovelock* [2007] EWCA Crim 476. See also *Stokes* [2015] EWCA Crim 1911, [21] where the Court disagreed that any false impression had been given at all; *Ovba* [2015] EWCA Crim 725, [8], where the impression D gave in evidence that she was a "*friendly person*" was "*far too unspecific and insubstantial*" to trigger gateway (f). Cases where the existence of a false impression is doubtful: *Bernasconi* [2006] EWCA Crim 1052; *Jarvis* [2008] EWCA Crim 488; *Eyidah* [2010] EWCA Crim 987.

In *Good*, the defendant was not given an opportunity to clarify whether he was asserting something or not, which led to his conviction being quashed.[303]

The defendant in *D, P and U* was convicted of the sexual abuse of his two stepsons. He had stated in interview that he "*preferred females*", but then asked the judge to edit that statement out of the interview so that it would not be adduced. He wished to withdraw any false impression about his sexual preferences that he had given in the interview. The judge refused, saying "*[e]ven if it were edited out, it does not alter the fact that that is what the defendant said and that was his reaction when these allegations were put to him.*" The Court of Appeal corrected this: "*That proposition fell into error because it ignores section 105(3). It also ignores the central proposition to be found in section 105(1)(a) that gateway (f) arises when a false impression is given to the court*",[304] which is to say that it can be prevented from being *given* to the court.

The proper application of s.105(3) was recently confirmed in *Khan*, where D's denial in interview that he supplied drugs was given in the context of being accused of selling drugs in a hostel. This was still capable of being a false impression, because "*to the extent that it was an implied assertion that he was not the sort of person who would ever supply another with Class A drugs, it was untrue.*" But the Court said, quashing the conviction,[305]

> *"In these circumstances, we can see no good reason why the record of the interview could not have been further edited, under section 105(6), so as to remove references to any more general implied assertion that he was not the sort of person who supplied drugs, so as to correct any false impression. … Nor do we understand why the judge thought that the evidence would be bound to come out. It was certainly not in the interests of the appellant to raise it, and we cannot*

303 *Good* [2008] EWCA Crim 2923.

304 *D, P and U* [2011] EWCA Crim 1474, [2012] 1 Cr App R 8, [39]. See also *Livesey* [2007] EWCA Crim 361, involving the withdrawal of a planned character statement once the defendant was informed that this would trigger gateway (f).

305 On this basis and on the basis of a separate misdirection to the jury.

> *see how the prosecution could have put questions with the intention of eliciting a damaging admission which would introduce the appellant's previous conviction."*[306]

The principle in s.105(3) would seem straightforward, except for cases such as *H*,[307] where the Court refused to allow the defendant to edit an interview record to remove the false impression he was alleged to have made, so as to avoid his convictions being put in evidence. Yet it would seem that s.105(3) is intended to do exactly this. Similarly, in *Dixon* the Court of Appeal stated:

> *"We reject [the defendant's] assertion that the proper way to correct any false impression created by the appellant in interview was to edit the interview. This is to miss the point. The evidence of what he had said when confronted by the allegations was relevant and admissible. If an accused lies in interview and the consequences for the appellant are unfortunate, the answer is not to edit out those lies. The answer is that the prosecution is entitled to rely upon those lies."*[308]

The purpose and effect of s.105(3) does not support this interpretation. It might be that these cases are outliers, given the rest of the case law. In so far as gateway (f) and false impressions are concerned, the "*proper way*" is indeed to edit the interview or otherwise to allow the defendant to withdraw or disassociate from the "*lie*" in the interview. The Explanatory Notes make it clear that the defendant was not intended to be allowed to use s.101(3) to request the exclusion of gateway (f) evidence, because he can achieve the same effect by withdrawing or disassociating himself from the false impression.[309] Exclusion, then, is the function of s.105(3). Of course, this does not prevent another gateway from operating to allow

---

306 *Khan* [2020] EWCA Crim 163, [20].

307 *H* [2006] EWCA Crim 2898.

308 *Dixon* [2012] EWCA Crim 2163, [17].

309 Explanatory Notes to the CJA, [378]: "*A defendant may withdraw or disassociate himself from a false or misleading impression. Evidence to correct the impression is not then admissible: section 105(3). In light of this, section 101(3), under which a defendant may apply to have evidence of his bad character excluded, does not apply to this evidence.*"

those convictions into evidence, provided that gateway's conditions are satisfied, as in fact happened in *Dixon* (via gateway (g)).

4.6.3 How Much Evidence Is Required To Correct A False Impression?

It has already been observed that gateway (f) lends itself to a circularity of use. The possibility was mentioned in *D, P and U*,[310] and can be observed in *Gillespie*.[311] There, the defendant was held to have given a false impression in respect of other bad character evidence which was already going to be admitted via gateway (d). This suggests a potential cyclical use of s.101. In that sense, there is no limit on gateway (f) (as there is on gateways (c), (d) and (e)), that the false impression or the bad character evidence has to be relevant to the trial.

There is one limit, however, that is important and unusual. It is that the scope and application of any evidence admitted via gateway (f) is very specific—it can only be evidence that has probative value in correcting the false impression, and may not go any further than is necessary to correct that false impression.[312] Bad character, therefore, is divisible for the purposes of gateway (f).[313] In order to comply with s.105(6), references to bad character should be removed where appropriate.[314]

The application of s.105(6) is fairly wide.

In *Uyiekpen*, the defendant's conviction for possessing class A drugs with intent to supply was quashed because the defendant had not been permitted to give evidence that he had no convictions for drug-related offences. The fact that he had a conviction for assault, and was facing trial on charges of robbery and false imprisonment, did not detract from the

[310] *D, P and U* [2011] EWCA Crim 1474, [2012] 1 Cr App R 8, [39].

[311] *Gillespie* [2011] EWCA Crim 3152.

[312] Section 105(1)(b) and (6).

[313] *Weir* [2005] EWCA Crim 2866, [2006] 1 Cr App R 19, [43]: "*We accept that [s 105(6)] is a statutory reversal of the previous common law position that character is indivisible*".

[314] *Lovelock* [2007] EWCA Crim 476.

accuracy of the assertion that he had no drug-related convictions. It was not a false impression to state that he had no previous convictions relating to drugs, and evidence of some pending charges "*was simply not admissible.*"[315]

In *Spartley*, the defendant said in interview that he had "*not been in trouble with police before and would not involve himself in an enterprise of the kind suggested*" (importation of drugs).[316] Evidence was admitted via gateway (f) to the effect that, seven years previously, he had been interviewed by Dutch police in relation to a cannabis investigation. No charges or convictions resulted. Was this a gateway (f) case? Arguably, the defendant did give a false impression because he essentially stated that he would not involve himself in an enterprise involving drug importation or supply. Were it not for this, the admission of the Dutch evidence relies upon "*trouble with the police*" being interpreted to include an interview from which no charges resulted. On a favourable interpretation of gateway (f), the defendant was merely saying that he had not previously been arrested, perhaps by the UK police.

An opposite result in *Wylie* suggests that these subtle distinctions may well be permissible, and even necessary, under gateway (f).[317] The defendant had never been arrested or interviewed by the police before, but he did have a conviction for a company-related offence that had been investigated by the Official Receiver. Thus, it was agreed with the prosecution that the defendant could say, when asked, that he had never been in trouble *with the police* before.[318] This would not trigger gateway (f).

If such a distinction can be made in *Wylie*, then presumably the opposite distinction can also be made (in a case such as *Spartley*) between different

---

315 *Uyiekpen* [2008] EWCA Crim 1457, [13].

316 *Spartley* [2007] EWCA Crim 1789, [14]. These are the Court's words—the exact phrase used in interview was not quoted.

317 *Wylie* [2010] EWCA Crim 3110.

318 Unfortunately, when he was actually questioned about the periphery of the previous matter, the defendant answered that he had "*never been in trouble before*", rather than that he had "*never been in trouble with the police before*"! The prosecution was then permitted to adduce details of the previous conviction.

police forces and, even, the subject of that "*trouble*", whether it is mere questioning, arrest or a formal charge.

A partial qualification to the divisibility of character is the scenario in *H*, where, on trial for murder, D give evidence in-chief of his practice of buying and selling stolen cars. In light of his lengthy record of more serious offences, including offences of serious violence and possession of bladed articles, the impression D had given about his bad character was misleading. A number (not all) of those serious convictions were therefore admissible under gateway (f).[319]

Finally, in *Omotoso*, the defendant's mis-statement in examination-in-chief as to the nature of his work did not convey a false impression that needed to be corrected by any bad character evidence. "*If there was real and justifiable concern about what [D] had said and the impression it might have conveyed, it could and should have been corrected in some form of admission as to what he had been doing*", which was unrelated to his bad character.[320] Further, the prosecution should have made any gateway (f) argument while the defendant was still giving evidence, and not after the defence had closed its case.

4.7 Gateway (g): S.101(1)(g)

"(g) the defendant has made an attack on another person's character"

"106 'Attack on another person's character'

> *(1) For the purposes of section 101(1)(g) a defendant makes an attack on another person's character if—*
>
> > *(a) he adduces evidence attacking the other person's character,*
> >
> > *(b) he (or any legal representative appointed under section 38(4) of the Youth Justice and Criminal*

319 *H* [2018] EWCA Crim 2868, [2019] 1 Cr App R 25.

320 *Omotoso* [2018] EWCA Crim 1394, [51].

Evidence Act 1999 (c. 23) to cross-examine a witness in his interests) asks questions in cross-examination that are intended to elicit such evidence, or are likely to do so, or

(c) evidence is given of an imputation about the other person made by the defendant—

(i) on being questioned under caution, before charge, about the offence with which he is charged, or

(ii) on being charged with the offence or officially informed that he might be prosecuted for it.

(2) In subsection (1) 'evidence attacking the other person's character' means evidence to the effect that the other person—

(a) has committed an offence (whether a different offence from the one with which the defendant is charged or the same one), or

(b) has behaved, or is disposed to behave, in a reprehensible way; and 'imputation about the other person' means an assertion to that effect.

(3) Only prosecution evidence is admissible under section 101(1)(g)."

4.7.1 Credibility

Gateway (g) contains no express reason for the admission of the bad character evidence. That the other substantive gateways do is clear from their wording: gateways (c), (d), (e) and (f) begin with reference to evidence of the defendant's bad character (they all begin with "*it*"), followed by some reason why that evidence is admissible. But gateway (g) makes no reference to the evidence. Nor does s.106.

Its predecessor, the second part of s.1(1)(f)(ii) of the Criminal Evidence Act 1898, reads, in context:

> *"A person charged in criminal proceedings who is called as a witness in the proceedings shall not be asked, and if asked shall not be required to answer, any question tending to show that he has committed or been convicted of or been charged with any offence other than one with which he is then charged, or is of bad character, unless ... the nature or conduct of the defence is such as to involve imputations on the character of the prosecutor or the witnesses for the prosecution."*

The case law on this provision indicated that the purpose of tit-for-tat character attacks was to level the playing field between the credibility of two witnesses: a defendant who gives evidence and the prosecution witness whose character he attacks.[321]

The idea of evening-out the playing field is still the central purpose of gateway (g).[322] Although there is nothing in the words of gateway (g) or s.106 to suggest it, the gateway has become, by default, about the defendant's own credibility. Thus: if the jury does not have character information for *both* sides in a credibility assessment task, the verdict may be unsafe.

---

321 This guide has not dwelt on pre-CJA law for obvious reasons. Most old cases are now no longer helpful: in *Littlechild* [2006] EWCA Crim 2126 the Court said it was "*very dangerous*" to interpret gateway (g) using the pre-CJA case of *Selvey v DPP* [1970] AC 304. See also *Platt* [2016] EWCA Crim 4, [23]-[29].

322 E.g. *McPherson* [2010] EWCA Crim 2906, [12].

Not everything a defendant says or asserts means that the playing field has been tilted in his favour.[323] The tit-for-tat approach should be used only where it is "*truly required*".[324]

In *Williams*, although the judge did not "*focus as clearly as he might on the distinction between 101(1)(d) and 101(1)(g)*", his decision to admit offences of dishonesty was correct.

> "*In a case where the defence had launched an attack on the character of the prosecution witnesses the jury were entitled to know about the character of the defendant and in particular that he had offences of dishonesty in deciding whether or not to believe his evidence rather than that of the prosecution witnesses.*"[325]

In *Brewster*, the Court allowed an appeal against convictions for kidnapping and theft, on the basis that the judge should have admitted evidence of the complainant's bad character, including a conviction for manslaughter. If this had been done, the defendants' bad character would also have been put into evidence, each having "*criminal records of some seriousness*".[326] It was very possible that "*if the jury had learned of the convictions of each of the main actors at trial*" they would have reached a different verdict. "*[T]he jury might have been persuaded that they could not safely act*

[323] It might be argued that a defendant is the first victim of the tit-for-tat game: he comes to trial only because the prosecutor has chosen to make an attack on his character (i.e. accusing him of a crime). The presumption of innocence is there to remind the tribunal of fact to avoid placing the accused in a disadvantaged position because of the fact that he has been accused.

[324] Lord Hope in *DS v Her Majesty's Advocate* [2007] UKPC 36, [43] said, when looking for comparative guidance from the legislation of England and Wales, that "*the court is required by that scheme to have regard to certain specific factors designed to* limit *the introduction of evidence on a tit-for-tat basis to those cases where it is truly required*" (emphasis added).

[325] *Williams* [2007] EWCA Crim 1951, [28]; and see *O'Sullivan* [2013] EWCA Crim 43, [19]. But see *Hearne* [2009] EWCA Crim 103.

[326] *Brewster* [2010] EWCA Crim 1194, [2010] 2 Cr App R 20, [25].

on [the complainant's] evidence notwithstanding the bad character of the accused."[327]

Note that gateway (g) does not require that anyone gives evidence before it is triggered. However, where the attack is on a non-witness who is also a non-victim, s.101(3) should normally be exercised to exclude the evidence.[328]

Even if gateway (g) is triggered, it does not follow that all aspects of D's bad character must be admitted. The judge can and should consider exclusion of each item of bad character under the exclusionary provisions (see Chapter 5). For example, in *Guthrie*, D's allegation that C had invented the whole incident meant that his "*entire character was capable of being adduced under (g)*", but "*[i]n order to avoid undue prejudice however the learned judge fairly ruled that offences relating to driving and dishonesty would not be admitted.*"[329]

4.7.2 Using Evidence After Admission

Balancing credibility is not the sole purpose of gateway (g).

Highton was asked to address the question:

> *"whether evidence admitted under s.101(1)(g) … is admissible as evidence of a propensity to commit offences of the kind with which the defendant is charged, or is only admissible in relation to his credibility, that is, as evidence tending to show that he is likely to be untruthful."*[330]

In response, the Court held that bad character evidence admitted via gateway (g) can be used for whatever relevant purpose exists.

> *"In the case of gateway (g), for example, admissibility depends on the defendant having made an attack on another person's*

327 *Brewster* [2010] EWCA Crim 1194, [2010] 2 Cr App R 20, [25].

328 *Nelson* [2006] EWCA Crim 3412, [16].

329 *Guthrie* [2016] EWCA Crim 1633, [14].

330 *Highton* [2005] EWCA Crim 1985, [2006] 1 Cr App R 7, [1].

> *character, but once the evidence is admitted, it may, depending on the particular facts, be relevant not only to credibility but also to propensity to commit offences of the kind with which the defendant is charged."*[331]

Highton therefore tells us that gateway (g) evidence can be relevant to propensity. It will not always be relevant.[332]

Thus, for example:

- Gateway (a) evidence can be used for both s.103(1)(a) and (b) types of propensity.[333] As to *Highton* and gateways (a) and (b) more generally, see above.

- Gateway (d) evidence can be used as gateway (c) evidence, where (c) was not otherwise satisfied: *Doncaster*.[334]

- Gateway (d) evidence can be used towards credibility in the gateway (g) sense, where a separate gateway (g) argument was rejected.[335]

---

331 *Highton* [2005] EWCA Crim 1985, [2006] 1 Cr App R 7, [10]. This last is a reference to the gateway (d) matter in issue of propensity (s.103(1)(a)).

332 *Williams* [2011] EWCA Crim 2198, [14]. The convictions in question were "*relevant to the purpose for which they were sought to be admitted under gateway (g)*" (i.e. whether the defendant was more worthy of belief than the police officers whose character he had attacked), but were not, and could not have been, relied upon as evidence of propensity. However, "*there was a clear and considerable risk of the jury treating them as such once the jury knew about them.*"

333 *Gourde* [2009] EWCA Crim 1803. This case shows it is advisable to agree the exact uses of the evidence before agreeing to use gateway (a).

334 *Doncaster* [2008] EWCA Crim 5.

335 *Hassett* [2008] EWCA Crim 1634, [29]: A credibility use is equivalent to a gateway (g) use. The judge directed "*that the convictions ... go not only to propensity but also to credibility*", which the Court of Appeal said meant "*that which had been admitted by reference to gateway (d) [as going to propensity] was also relevant now to gateway (g) [thus going also to credibility]. There is authority permitting such an approach: see* R v Highton".

- Evidence admitted as relevant to one important matter in issue (under gateway (d)) can then be used for another gateway (d) purpose even if it would not have been admissible for that second purpose. In *Campbell* the important matter in issue was a propensity to commit domestic violence offences. The bad character evidence could then be used for a credibility purpose, not because s.103(1)(b) was satisfied (it was not) but because "*[o]nce the evidence has been admitted through a gateway it is open to the jury to attach significance to it in any respect in which it is relevant.*"[336] This is subject to the important requirement that the court must decide what those relevant uses are and must direct the jury on them.[337]

The *Highton* principle is not clear-cut. *Highton* arose because the Court was asked whether evidence admitted under gateway (g) can be used, for example, for a gateway (d) purpose. Because the other gateways generally have readily-identifiable parameters (unlike gateway (g)), it is not always appropriate to ask whether evidence admitted via those gateways can be used for a different purpose.

As a result, many cases limit or contradict the above uses.[338] For example:

- The judge retains the power to confine the uses of the evidence.[339]

- Evidence admitted under gateway (c) should not readily be used for a purpose such as propensity for which additional safeguards and different tests have first to be met.[340]

---

336 *Campbell* [2007] EWCA Crim 1472, [2007] 2 Cr App R 28, [25].

337 *D, P and U* [2011] EWCA Crim 1474, [2012] 1 Cr App R 8, [3].

338 There are many texts discussing whether *Highton* was correctly decided. This text confines such discussion to practical points that may assist.

339 *Lamaletie and Royce* [2008] EWCA Crim 314, [13].

340 *Davis* [2008] EWCA Crim 1156, [2009] 2 Cr App R 17, [34]. *Davis* is suggesting that the *Highton* approach is only permissible if the admitting gateway is more stringent than the gateway(s) that would lead to different usages. Thus a party cannot use an

- A judge who is minded to direct the jury that a conviction is relevant to propensity must apply the principles in *Hanson*.[341] This would seem to narrow *Highton* considerably.

- Gateways (d) and (e) have separate identities, specify a standard of relevance to something[342] and by default should be used for that purpose.[343]

- Gateway (f) evidence is particularly unlikely to be capable of any other uses. In *Parsons* D's previous convictions had been admitted under gateway (f) to rebut his false assertion in chief that he had never been to court before. There was a potential other usage because one conviction was for possession of cannabis, and the present charge was for supplying cannabis. The Court of Appeal held that the judge should have directed the jury that the convictions could not be used for a s.103(1)(a) propensity purpose, and that the convictions were only before the jury in order to "*cure the false impression*".[344] There was no mention of *Highton* at all.

---

easier gateway to allow a usage that belongs to a more difficult gateway. It seeks to confine *Highton* to situations where admissibility is achieved via gateways (d) and (g) only. In the situation of gateway (c), while "*it would seem difficult to think that the jury should be limited in its use*", there is also a "*danger*" in admitting evidence via gateway (c) if the intended use is really as evidence of propensity, "*where the statutory tests and safeguards are different*" at [36]. The Court then cites a number of cases for the proposition that gateway (c) should not be subject to the *Highton* principle.

341 *Fryer and Tedstone* [2006] EWCA Crim 1530.

342 E.g. an important matter in issue.

343 *Lawson* [2006] EWCA Crim 2572, [2007] 1 Cr App R 11, [35] described the differences between gateways (d) and (e): "*It is quite apparent from the shape of this Act that although it uses the expression 'propensity for untruthfulness' in both section 103(1)(b) in relation to prosecution applications and in section 104(1) in relation to applications by co-accused, it addresses the various different occasions on which bad character may arguably be admissible separately and provides a* different framework of rules for each situation" (emphasis added). See also *Singh* [2007] EWCA Crim 2140, [9]: "*The Act plainly demonstrates that the gateways are independent, although of course in some cases more than one of them may be passed.*"

344 *Parsons* [2011] EWCA Crim 2591. See also *Cudjoe* [2012] EWCA Crim 3062, [15]-[17]; *Weir* [2005] EWCA Crim 2866, [2006] 1 Cr App R 19, [43].

It might be inferred that the Court considered that s.105(6) negated any applicability of *Highton*. Gateway (f) has an explicit *limitation* on the scope of the evidence and its usage. Section 105(6) in fact links the question of 'admissibility' with that of 'usage': if the evidence could go (meaning could 'achieve', or 'be used for') further than is necessary to correct the false impression, then it is not even admissible.

- The prosecution should not ordinarily seek to use *Highton* to rely on evidence that has been admitted by a defendant via gateway (e) or (c). When D2 adduces evidence of D1's bad character, "*it is to be hoped that the prosecution do not seek in closing the case to the jury to rely on it*",[345] unless the evidence is also admissible via a prosecution gateway. This principle was not followed in *Stokes* where, apparently by agreement, evidence admitted under gateway (e) could be used by all parties "*as they sought fit*", despite a prosecution application to admit the same bad character evidence having earlier been refused.[346]

- *Highton* "*does not relieve the court of the duty of establishing which gateway or gateways are applicable*",[347] because (1) this ensures that bad character evidence "*is only admitted when the statute allows it*", and (2) because "*the decision as to the relevant gateway or gateways will normally be of great help in identifying the way or ways in which the evidence can legitimately be used—that is to say the issues to which it is relevant.*" This ensures that the evidence is used only "*on any issue to which it is legitimately relevant*", and not merely "*in any way the jury chooses.*" The application of these principles is clear in the case of *D*.[348] The bad character evidence undoubtedly passed gateway (g), but because it had the potential to be used for propensity purposes as well, gateway (d) needed to be

---

345 *Robinson* [2005] EWCA Crim 3233, [2006] 1 Cr App R 32.

346 *Stokes* [2018] EWCA Crim 1350, [29].

347 *D, P and U* [2011] EWCA Crim 1474, [2012] 1 Cr App R 8, [3].

348 *D, P and U* [2011] EWCA Crim 1474, [2012] 1 Cr App R 8, beginning at [24].

considered. This would allow the judge to determine how the jury should be directed.

Arguably, *Highton* is needed only in those situations where the gateway (g) usage is unclear, or where there is an unavoidable overlap between the gateway (g) usage and the gateway (d) conditions.

Thus, in *Lafayette* the Court distinguished the situation where bad character evidence admitted under gateway (g) is also admissible under gateway (d) (meaning that both sets of *admission* criteria are satisfied), from the situation where evidence admissible under gateway (g) is not admissible under gateway (d) to show propensity.

> *In many cases at least some of the bad character evidence admitted under gateway (g) will also be admissible under gateway (d) and thus entitle the judge to give a propensity direction (see* Highton *…). What is the position to-day if the evidence which is admissible under gateway (g) is not admissible under gateway (d) to show propensity? For example, what should the judge say if the evidence under gateway (g) showed only previous convictions for offences of dishonesty and/or drugs offences and/or offences of violence, from any of which the jury would not be entitled to conclude that they showed on the part of the defendant a propensity to commit the kind of offences with which he is charged?*[349]

The first situation entitles the judge to give a propensity direction, whereas the second does not. *"[T]he better course is for the direction to be so fashioned in a gateway (g) only case that the jury understand that the relevance of these kinds of previous convictions goes to credit and they should not consider that it shows a propensity to commit the offence they are considering, at least if there is a risk that they might do so."*

Chrysostomou expounds a cautious approach to usage after gateway (g) (in particular requiring some probative value beyond blackening the defendant's general character): *"In our view, the texts had no relevance other than*

[349] *Lafayette* [2008] EWCA Crim 3238, [49].

to blacken the general character of the appellant in the eyes of the jury and, therefore, dent the credibility of his evidence generally."[350]

The problem of gateway (g) might be said to be captured by the direction in *Noble*:

> *"Now, you heard about [D's bad character], members of the jury, because there have been attacks on the characters of prosecution witnesses in this case. And in those circumstances, it is only right that you should hear something of the character of the persons making that attack. But you may feel, members of the jury, that in the context of this case—given firstly that those matters were a long time ago where [D] would have been very young—they do not add anything to this case. And you may think in the circumstances that you can ignore them. Certainly, members of the jury, you must not assume in any way that a defendant is guilty just because he has previous convictions. And you may think that in the circumstances here, as I say, they do not take the matter any further at all."*[351]

In light of that assessment, it might be queried what the purpose of admitting this evidence was.

Given the variety of approaches above, it is good practice to consider whether the use of gateway (g) evidence for additional purposes is compatible with a fair trial and will not distract the jury from the main issues in the case.

There may remain a power to exclude evidence.[352]

4.7.3 What Is Evidence Attacking Another Person's Character?

This largely mirrors the definition of bad character given by s.98 and s.112(1), except that there is no s.98(a) equivalent

---

350 *Chrysostomou* [2010] EWCA Crim 1403, [40].

351 *Noble* [2016] EWCA Crim 2219, [80].

352 See Chapter 5 gateway (g) discussion.

Section 106(1)(a) refers to "*evidence attacking the other person's character*".

This is defined in s.106(2) as:

1. Evidence "*to the effect that*" the other person has committed an offence.
    a. This offence can be any conviction or allegation.
    b. It can include the offence with which the defendant is charged.
2. Evidence "*to the effect that*" the other person has behaved or is disposed to behave in a reprehensible way. The meaning of "*reprehensible*" should be interpreted in line with the definition of "*misconduct*" in s.112(1).[353]
3. An "*imputation*" about a person means an assertion to that effect. This is intended to capture mere allegations, accusations, and otherwise unsupported statements about a person.[354] No proof from the defendant as to the accusation is required before gateway (g) is triggered.

An important note about the above definition is that it does not exclude evidence that falls within s.98(a). Thus, an attack on someone's character that is to do with the alleged facts of the offence (typically, if the defendant accuses the complainant of lying, or of initiating a fight) can still trigger gateway (g). Whether it *should* do so in any individual case will be a matter for argument. Section 101(3) should be used to avoid unfairness towards a defendant who reasonably needs to make such accusations in pursuit of his defence.

[353] See Chapter 2.

[354] E.g. that a witness was "*evil, vindictive and violent, she drank too much, had a vendetta against him, told malicious lies about him, and had even taken out a contract on his life*": *JP* [2016] EWCA Crim 1331, [50].

In *Yaryare*, the Court held that cross-examination of a police officer which suggested that the officer's evidence was in part "*false or based on deliberately exaggerated testimony*", and that she was "*intent on getting a conviction and keeping her reputation intact*" was sufficient to trigger gateway (g).[355]

A somewhat different approach was taken in *Walker*. D was on trial for the manslaughter of a baby, and sought in interview to blame a paramedic for the death. The judge was "*was not persuaded that it would be right*" to admit D's bad character under gateway (g).[356]

Similarly, in *Omotoso*, the Court said:

> *"It may be that cross-examination of a police officer to suggest that his investigation was flawed may amount to an attack on his character, but judges should be careful to ensure that gateway (g) is not invoked too lightly in such cases, and thereby inhibit a legitimate line of questioning. A gentle hint should be sufficient to alert trial counsel of the potential dangers of pursuing a particular course. Although the Judge recognised that undermining a police officer's evidence might be legitimate, he drew a distinction where it went 'beyond the issues in the case'. Plainly gratuitous insults should not be permitted in the course of cross-examination and may lead to the revelation of the defendant's character under gateway (g), but the Judge gave no examples of how the questioning suggested that the officer failed to do his job properly or how the cross-examination went beyond the issues in the case."*[357]

4.7.4 How Is An Attack Made?

An attack on another person's character can be made in a number of ways:

---

355 *Yaryare* [2020] EWCA Crim 1314, [2020] 4 WLR 156, [101]-[102].

356 *Walker* [2019] EWCA Crim 1825, [23].

357 *Omotoso* [2018] EWCA Crim 1394, [59].

- A direct attack by evidence: s.106(1)(a). E.g. giving oral evidence that 'person A has a conviction for assault'. This is the most common way of attacking someone else's character and makes the triggering of gateway (g) obvious.

- Cross-examining a witness (on behalf of the defendant) in such a way as to elicit an attack on someone's character: s.106(1)(b). Thus, asking a police officer, 'Can you confirm that witness A has a conviction for assault?' This provision is rarely used without an agreed position being discussed in advance (i.e. D agrees to sacrifice his shield in exchange for this evidence). The words at the end of s.106(1)(b), "*or are likely to do so*", are not of much assistance. They cover the circumstance where the content of the attack is evident from the question but the witness does not actually give the desired answer.

- Evidence is given at trial of an imputation the defendant made about the other person before the trial. Commonly, this covers the situation where the defendant alleges something about person A during his police interview or upon charge. The key here is that the evidence of that imputation needs to be "*given*" at the trial. It is not enough that the defendant *made* the imputation. This is akin to the gateway (f) provision which states that a false impression can be withdrawn and not relied upon.

An attack must be made in the presence of the jury. Statements made on behalf of the defence in the absence of the jury (e.g. in an abuse argument) cannot form the basis of an argument under gateway (g).[358]

In *Nelson* the Court held that the judge was wrong to allow gateway (g) to apply to the defendant's comments in a police interview, because they were not relevant and should not have been admitted. The judge did not properly address why the defendant's objection to the "*giving*" of the evidence should not be upheld.

---

[358] *Omotoso* [2018] EWCA Crim 1394, [53].

> *"It is, in our view, difficult to see what relevance to the issues before the jury the appellant's comments in interview about [the victim's friend] could have had. Certainly it would be improper for the prosecution to seek to get such comments before a jury simply to provide a basis for satisfying gateway (g) and getting the defendant's previous convictions put in evidence. We do not seek to suggest that that was the motivation of the prosecution in this case but nonetheless, objectively speaking, that seems to us to have been the situation which arose. It follows that, in our judgment, this was not a proper basis for meeting the requirements of gateway (g) on admissibility."*[359]

However, contrast *Hanson* (*Pickstone*) where D made a character attack on C in interview, which the Court described as a "*self-serving assertion*":

> *"Nor do we accept that the evidence had to be excluded because the defendant was not warned at the time of the interview of the possible consequences of what he said. Anyone who makes a self-serving assertion of significance in interview can expect the Crown to seek to adduce, at the subsequent trial, relevant and admissible evidence to refute it. In this case, that included the evidence of the defendant's earlier conviction."*[360]

Of course, such warnings are not required at police stations (unlike s.34 warnings under the Criminal Justice and Public Order Act 1994 (CJPOA)). It might seem harsh that a defendant cannot choose to resile from what may have been an unguarded or heated accusation that he does not now rely on at trial.

Note that there is no requirement that the attack made by the defendant is unjust or unfounded. The statement that triggers gateway (g) might be

---

[359] *Nelson* [2006] EWCA Crim 3412, [19].

[360] *Hanson* [2005] EWCA Crim 824, [2005] 2 Cr App R 21, [52]. However, note that an attack on another is not always "*a self-serving assertion*".

completely accurate and undisputed. This does not protect the defendant against the admission of his own bad character.

Merely putting a defence (as opposed to making gratuitous attacks that have limited relevance) can still cause a defendant to lose his shield. In *Benabbou*, the Court agreed that the defence case unavoidably involved attacking prosecution witnesses, and that this also ran the inevitable risk of facilitating admission of a prior conviction.[361] An exclusionary provision such as s.101(3) should play a role here to prevent tactical unfairness to the defendant.[362]

However, a distinction should be drawn between the *Benabbou* scenario and a case where the defence merely calls or relies on evidence that undermines or is inconsistent with what a prosecution witness has said.[363] The latter is not an attack that triggers gateway (g).

361 *Benabbou* [2012] EWCA Crim 1256, [28].

362 See its importance in *Omotoso* [2018] EWCA Crim 1394, [61]-[62].

363 *Omotoso* [2018] EWCA Crim 1394, [60], referring to the calling of evidence that "*was intended to undermine the evidence of the officer in the case*".

CHAPTER FIVE

EXCLUSIONS

This Chapter deals with the exclusion of bad character evidence that has passed the initial admissibility test (i.e. a gateway in Chapters 3 and 4). It focuses on the statutory exclusions for prosecution evidence, and then deals with some specific issues arising in respect of defence evidence. It also examines the remedial or exclusionary options provided by s.107 and s.108.

The only formal exclusions are those in s.101(3)/s.101(4) and s.103(3).

However, s.78 of PACE is also applicable to prosecution evidence.

There are no formal exclusionary provisions in relation to bad character evidence admitted at the behest of a non-prosecution party. Gateway (e) has a pseudo-exclusion, dealt with at the end of this Chapter.

5.1 Statutory Provisions

Section 101(3) reads:

> *"The court must not admit evidence under subsection (1)(d) or (g) if, on an application by the defendant to exclude it, it appears to the court that the admission of the evidence would have such an adverse effect on the fairness of the proceedings that the court ought not to admit it."*

Section 101(4) elaborates:

> *"On an application to exclude evidence under subsection (3) the court must have regard, in particular, to the length of time between the matters to which that evidence relates and the matters which form the subject of the offence charged."*

Section 103(3) reads:

> *"(3) Subsection (2) [referring to a defendant's propensity to commit offences of the kind with which he is charged] does not apply in the case of a particular defendant if the court is satisfied, by reason of the length of time since the conviction or for any other reason, that it would be unjust for it to apply in his case."*

Section 78 reads:

> *"Exclusion of unfair evidence*
>
> *(1) In any proceedings the court may refuse to allow evidence on which the prosecution proposes to rely to be given if it appears to the court that, having regard to all the circumstances, including the circumstances in which the evidence was obtained, the admission of the evidence would have such an adverse effect on the fairness of the proceedings that the court ought not to admit it.*
>
> *(2) Nothing in this section shall prejudice any rule of law requiring a court to exclude evidence."*

By s.112(1), *"prosecution evidence"* means evidence which is to be (or has been) adduced by the prosecution, or which a witness is to be invited to give (or has given) in cross-examination by the prosecution.

5.2 Section 78 Of PACE

Summary:

- If seeking to exclude bad character evidence, it is advisable to rely on s.101(3) instead of s.78 for gateways (d) and (g).[364] Both can

[364] Because the power in s.101(3) is explicit and refers only to two gateways, it may have been intended that there should be no other power that could disallow evidence admitted via any other gateway.

be argued, but as they largely duplicate the same concept, failure on one is likely to mean failure on the other.

- Section 78 can be used when the defendant wishes to oppose the prosecution's use of gateways (c) or (f) (as s.101(3) does not assist here).

- Section 78 applies to any prosecution evidence that falls within the s.98 exceptions (s.98(a) and (b)), as such evidence is not evidence of bad character.[365]

- Section 78 applies to prosecution evidence admitted under s.100.

- Gateway (e) cannot be subject to s.78, because it cannot be used to admit prosecution evidence.

5.2.1 Does S.101(3) Preclude The Use Of S.78?

Early cases were unclear on this point. In *Davis* the Court of Appeal said that "*the role of s.78 in relation to gateway (c) is possibly controversial*".[366]

However, the position is now clearer and s.78 is regularly used in respect of prosecution evidence of bad character, however admitted.

5.2.2 Differences Between S.78 And S.101(3)

Section 78 is broader (a generalised provision), designed to deal with any problem the court may face (including illegitimate means of obtaining evidence), whereas s.101(3) and (4) are tailored specifically to the use of bad character evidence, and contemplate the use of evidence that dates from some time in the past.

Section 101(3) requires an application by the defendant, whereas s.78 is a provision that should be in the court's contemplation at all times, even if it decides not to exercise the power therein. Similarly, s..103(3) is not

[365] *McPherson* [2010] EWCA Crim 2906, [16].

[366] *Davis* [2008] EWCA Crim 1156, [2009] 2 Cr App R 17, [36].

dependent upon application by the defendant.[367]

Section 78 is written in an optional style ("*may refuse*") whereas s.101(3) is mandatory ("*must not*"). *Hanson* suggests that s.101(3) is a stronger provision than s.78 PACE, because the words "*must not admit*" carry a greater imperative than "*may refuse to allow*".[368] On the other hand, the interpretation in *Tirnaveanu* of the pre-CJA case of *Chalkley* suggests that although s.78 ("*may refuse*") seems to import more discretion, both are still essentially mandatory provisions, containing the words "*ought not to admit*".[369] Most discussions tend to treat both provisions as equivalent. In *Malone* the Court of Appeal held that a s.78 ruling could be substituted for a missing s.101(3) ruling.[370]

In any case, *Hanson* does not tell us that s.78 no longer applies to any of the s.101(1) gateways. Other cases have since gone further. In *Highton* the Court of Appeal suggested, *obiter*, that s.78 applies to all of the s.101 gateways, a step that also allows the courts to avoid any risk of failing to comply with Article 6 of the European Convention on Human Rights.[371] "*[I]t is right that we should say that, without having heard full argument, our inclination is to say that s.78 provides an additional protection to a defendant.*"

This suggestion was given validity in *O'Dowd*, where the Court of Appeal said that s.78 also applies in the bad character context, and expressed

[367] Thus the defendant's request in *Miller* [2010] EWCA Crim 1578 that the judge not consider s.103(3) at all, for tactical reasons, causes some problems. *Miller* concerned the rape of the defendant's 11-year-old niece. While a teenager in 1997, the defendant was convicted of the gang rape of a 15-year-old acquaintance. The prosecution wished to use this conviction for s.103(1)(a) purposes. The defendant objected, but asked the judge to confine himself to the s.103(1)(a) propensity question and not to consider s.103(3) or PACE s.78. This was because the defendant wanted to suggest that his niece had made a false complaint against him while knowing that his 1997 conviction would support her.

[368] *Hanson* [2005] EWCA Crim 824, [2005] 2 Cr App R 21, [10].

[369] *Tirnaveanu* [2007] EWCA Crim 1239, [2007] 2 Cr App R 23, [28], citing *Chalkley & Jeffries* [1998] QB 848.

[370] *Malone* [2006] EWCA Crim 1860, [50].

[371] *Highton* [2005] EWCA Crim 1985, [2006] 1 Cr App R 7, [13]-[14].

doubt that this was even a "*controversial*" question any more.[372] A number of cases have since been very confident that s.78 should be applied when s.101(3) does not apply,[373] or even in conjunction with s.101(3).[374] Thus it can be used in both gateway (c)[375] and gateway (f) [376] circumstances. It can be used when multiple gateways are being relied upon, and for a mixture of bad character and non-bad character evidence, as in *Fox*: "*Were the evidence admissible under (d) the judge would have had to consider s.101(3). Furthermore, s.78 ... was also relevant when considering the cumulative effect of admitting more than one of the three categories of evidence*".[377]

A successful prosecution application to admit non-defendant bad character evidence under s.100 can still be subject to s.78.[378]

Therefore, the prudent view is likely to be that the court can and should

---

372 *O'Dowd* [2009] EWCA Crim 905, [2009] 2 Cr App R 16, [31].

373 *Edwards and Rowlands* [2005] EWCA Crim 3244, [2006] 2 Cr App R 4, [78] seems to assume that s.78 will apply if s.101(3) does not.

374 *Mustapha* [2007] EWCA Crim 1702, [22]: "*It is common ground that in addition to s.101(3) the court may consider the provisions of s.78 of PACE when deciding whether or not to rule evidence of bad character admissible*"; *Murphy* [2006] EWCA Crim 3408 (applied both s.101(3) and s.78); *Tirnaveanu* [2007] EWCA Crim 1239, [2007] 2 Cr App R 23, [27] (where s.101(3) cannot be relied on, use s.78).

375 *Bahaji* [2009] EWCA Crim 2863, [35] seems to assume that s.78 applies in gateway (c) circumstances. *Darnley* [2012] EWCA Crim 1148, [33] is probably incorrect in assuming that because s.101(3) does not apply to gateway (c), there is therefore no discretion to exclude evidence falling within that gateway. Section 78 would still apply as the prosecution adduced the evidence.

376 See, e.g., *Hickinbottom* [2012] EWCA Crim 783; *Weir* [2005] EWCA Crim 2866, [2006] 1 Cr App R 19, [44] (s.78 applied in gateway (f) circumstance (but did not help in that case)); *RB* [2008] EWCA Crim 1850, [33]; *Wylie* [2010] EWCA Crim 3110, [16] (seems to accept that s.78 could apply to gateway (f) but would not have helped in this particular case). In *Chrysostomou* [2010] EWCA Crim 1403 the choice was between gateways (g) and (f): "*Our conclusion above that the proper gateway in this case was only that in section 101(1)(g) means that we must focus on section 101(3) rather than section 78 of PACE 1984*" at [39]. However, this must by implication mean that if the proper gateway had been (f), s.78 would have applied.

377 *Fox* [2009] EWCA Crim 653, [28].

378 See, recently, *Boxall* [2020] EWCA Crim 688.

apply s.78 in all bad character cases when there is any uncertainty as to the effect of the evidence on the fairness of the proceedings.

5.2.3 Section 78 And Co-Defendants

Section 78 also has a role to play in the event that D2 wishes to object to the admission of evidence (at the prosecution's behest) of D1's bad character.

The wording of s.101(3) and s.103(3) would seem to preclude D2 making any representations under those provisions.

Section 101(3) requires "*application by the defendant*", which must mean the defendant to whom the bad character in s.101 applies. Possibly, if D1 applies to exclude, D2 could then make representations as to the "*adverse effect on the fairness of the proceedings*".

Section 103(3) refers specifically to "*the case of a particular defendant … unjust for it to apply* in his case." The court would appear to be precluded from considering any unjustness in the case of a defendant who is not the relevant defendant under s.103.

This leaves s.78 which is broad enough to encompass any prosecution evidence, does not require any party's application, and requires the court to look at the whole of the case including the effect on any co-defendants.

Section 78 of PACE may operate to exclude D2's guilty plea to the same offence. The principle in the pre-CJA case of *O'Connor* has been approved in subsequent cases.[379] D1 was tried for conspiracy. D2's guilty plea to the same offence was admitted, allowing the prosecution to rely on an untested statement which had been made by D2 in D1's absence. The Court said:

379 *O'Connor* (1987) 85 Cr App R 298, 302-303. See *Smith* [2007] EWCA Crim 2105, and the line of cases following it: *Stevens* [2020] EWCA Crim 280; *D* [2009] EWCA Crim 1361; *M v Uxbridge Magistrates' Court* [2010] EWHC 673 (Admin); *O'Brien* [2016] EWCA Crim 698. As to the use of s.74 and s.98(a), see Chapter 2.

> "*We find this a difficult point, and, without deciding the full scope of section 74 [for which now substitute s.98(a)], for the purposes of this case, it is sufficient to say that if it was appropriate within the section to admit the conviction of [the co-accused] in the proceedings, we take the view that it would have resulted in a very unfair state of affairs. ... section 78 ought to have been brought into play by the learned judge. This was a case in which the admission of the evidence would have such an adverse effect on the fairness of the proceedings that the court ought not to have admitted it.*"

The decision will depend on the facts, but it is suggested that there must be a compelling reason to admit such evidence.

5.3 Sections 101(3) And 103(3)

Section 101(3) provides an exclusion for gateways (d) and (g). It is duplicated, in a narrower fashion, for gateway (d) by s.103(3), but only where s.103(2) is being used.

These sections are not applicable to any other gateway.

Summary:

- Concepts of fairness and injustice in the exclusions are intended to guide the conclusion of the trial to a fair outcome. It is in all parties' interests that, if evidence of the defendant's bad character is to be used, that use should result in a fair conviction.

- The pre-CJA test that weighs the probative value of evidence against its prejudicial effect is not strictly applicable, but can be useful.

- There is no set rule about how long is too long between bad character evidence and the present offence.

- Broader principles about the lapse of time can apply to s.78 and other gateways as well.

- A very old conviction may still be admissible if something has happened between that conviction and the index offence that continues the propensity.

- Evidence of bad character that occurred *after* the present matter can also provide sufficient continuity to avoid s.101(3).

5.3.1 Preliminary Observations

What is "*fairness*" in s.101(3) and s.78?[380]

This is not as simple as fairness to both defence and prosecution. In *Tully and Wood* the judge allowed, and even encouraged, the admission of offences dating from when the defendant was 13 years old, because although they would be prejudicial, "*[f]airness, of course, involves fairness to both defence and to the prosecution.*"[381]

The Court of Appeal was critical of this approach, holding that the admission of this wide range of offences did threaten the fairness of the trial. It is not enough to say that it is fair to the prosecution to admit the evidence because causing prejudice to the defendant is an accepted consequence of admitting bad character evidence and one that Parliament intended.

In addition, it might even be said that s.101(3) and s.78 are only concerned with adverse effects on fairness from the point of view of the defendant. The language focuses upon adverse effects caused by *admission of prosecution evidence*: such evidence is normally adduced against the defendant, and thus the adverse effect would manifest in unfairness to the defendant.

Fairness is an overall assessment of the trial: it is in the interests of justice

---

[380] Section 103(3) refers not to fairness but to the injustice of allowing similar convictions to be used to establish the defendant's propensity to commit offences of the kind charged. It is possible that the same argument may be made in relation to the assessment of such injustice.

[381] *Tully and Wood* [2006] EWCA Crim 2270, [20]. See also *Miller* [2009] EWCA Crim 2890.

(not in the interests of only one party) to ensure that the proceedings, and any conviction, are fair. It is in all parties' interests that, if evidence of the defendant's bad character is to be used, that use should result in a fair conviction.

Do s.101(3), s.78, or s.103(3) include the pre-CJA test that weighs the probative value of evidence against its prejudicial effect?

They do not use the same words,[382] but the test is often still referred to, especially in the s.101(3) context.[383]

The Court of Appeal has said, "*[t]he purpose of the subsection [101(3)] is to ensure that evidence of bad character is not admitted unless it has sufficient probative value to outweigh any risk of prejudice to the defendant and does not affect the fundamental fairness of the proceedings.*"[384]

Prejudicial effect is what arises when evidence, particularly bad character evidence, is given *more* weight than it deserves. If the evidence is capable of enough logical and unemotional force—or probative value—then it should be used in that way, and will by definition not have an *unfair* adverse effect, and hence no prejudicial effect. In reality, it is impossible to know what weight the jury will give to bad character evidence. If it is of a particularly repellent kind, the jury may unconsciously feel that the defendant deserves some punishment, regardless of the probative value of the evidence.[385]

In general, as probative value increases, so too does its prejudicial effect against the defendant. When the fairness of the proceedings is at risk, it is likely that the prejudicial effect of the evidence is too great.

---

382 See also *Weir* [2005] EWCA Crim 2866, [2006] 1 Cr App R 19, [36].

383 E.g. *Mustapha* [2007] EWCA Crim 1702; *Adams* [2006] EWCA Crim 2013.

384 *Cortes Plaza* [2013] EWCA Crim 501, [26].

385 Known as "*forbidden reasoning*" or "*just deserts*" reasoning: see *DF* [2011] EWCA Crim 2168.

Note that, where cross-admissibility is concerned,[386] the exception in s.101(3) cannot apply, because the effect would be to exclude the evidence in question from the trial and create a severed indictment. For the same reason, presumably s.103(3) and s.78 cannot apply (although s.78 can still apply on general grounds).

Section 103(3) is very specific in its application and is not capable of responding to the 'unjustness' of any usage that is not triggered by sub-s 103(1)(a) and 103(2). That is, if conviction bad character evidence is being used to establish the defendant's propensity to commit offences of the kind with which he is charged, then s.103(3) may apply specifically to that method of establishing the propensity, but it will not apply to any other method or any usage other than establishing this propensity. As such it actually provides little protection.

5.3.2 Time: The General Principle

Time is a key principle in exclusion arguments.

There is no set rule for how long is too long. Case examples vary considerably.

Hanson generally regards the commission date "*of more significance than the date of conviction when assessing admissibility*".[387]

In *Adams* a time gap of 17 years (six years since conviction) was not obviously accounted for in the judge's reasoning. Approving an "*economical*"[388] trial judgment, the Court of Appeal did not summarise the judge's reasons for refusing to exclude the evidence, and it is not evident from the appeal judgment that the judge cited ss.101(3) and (4) or s.103(3). Indeed it would seem that the judge substituted for those provisions a "*familiar balancing exercise*" between probative value and prejudicial effect, a test that does not appear in the Act.

Contrast this with *Dhooper,* where the judge's failure to cite s.101(4)

[386] See Chapter 6.

[387] *Hanson* [2005] EWCA Crim 824, [2005] 2 Cr App R 21, [11].

[388] *Adams* [2006] EWCA Crim 2013, [12].

when refusing to exclude evidence of a 13-year-old conviction led to the appeal being allowed. The Court of Appeal said that although there was a possibility the judge had in mind s.101(4), this was not enough.

> *"S.101(4) is an important provision … It is essential for a court to have regard to the length of time particularly in cases where it is substantial … Moreover, it is not sufficient for a judge simply to state baldly that he or she has had regard to the length of the interval of time, in a case where the interval is a long one and where the risk that it will have an adverse effect on fairness may be a real one. … There was plainly a real risk in the present case that the length of time of 13 years would have such an effect. If the judge was proposing nevertheless to admit the evidence, he had to grapple with the length of time and explain why, despite the passage of 13 years, admission of the evidence would nevertheless not have an adverse effect on the fairness of the proceedings."*[389]

The Court of Appeal begins from the position that to admit the evidence will be problematic, and requires rigorous proof of any reasoning leading to a different conclusion.

It may be helpful to look to the underlying reason for the passage of time exclusion.

The point of interest is not time *per se*, but time *plus* opportunity. For example, two similar events (the first being an offence for which D was convicted, and the second the subject of the present charge) committed five years apart may be treated one way if the offender spent the intervening period in prison, but another way if he spent it in freedom in the community.[390] Of course, any benefits from the period of time in prison should be taken into account as well, for example the possibility of rehabilitation, reform and the likelihood of reoffending. The effect of the time gap also depends upon the type of crime the defendant is accused of

---

[389] *Dhooper* [2008] EWCA Crim 2892, [19].

[390] The time gap in *Jackson* [2007] EWCA Crim 1892 might have been addressed in this fashion.

having a propensity to commit. If the crime is incest, it is usually easy to identify a lack of opportunity, especially if the defendant has been in prison. But if it involves theft, assault or drug offences, the court should consider the opportunities the defendant had to commit further crimes in prison (where such crimes can be rife), and whether the defendant was involved in these or not. It could even be argued that courts should take into account the potential while imprisoned to become introduced to organised crime and further means of committing crimes.

Non-conviction bad character evidence is certainly very unlikely to pass s.101(3) and (4) if it is more than 20 years old.[391]

The question of time may be interpreted differently in different gateways.

Gateway (c). As observed in Chapter 4, temporally distant evidence will not usually satisfy gateway (c). In *O*, evidence dated six months before the event charged was not too remote for gateway (d) purposes, but would have been unlikely to satisfy gateway (c).[392]

In the context of gateway (c) it need only be observed that the question whether evidence B can provide a sufficiently valuable explanation for evidence A can often be influenced by the comparative ages of each piece of evidence. This is not *always* true, for a vital explanation may originate in events taking place many years earlier. Time, therefore, is an incidental consideration for the purposes of gateway (c). As was said in *Davis*:

> *"It will be observed that admission under gateway (d), where it is disputed, requires the court to consider the effect on the fairness of the proceedings, in particular by reference to the age of the bad character in question. Such considerations do not apply to gateway (c). That is because its legitimacy is established by reference to its own rationale and purpose, that is to say the necessity for such evidence, since without it the*

[391] *Davis* [2008] EWCA Crim 1156, [2009] 2 Cr App R 17.

[392] *O* [2010] EWCA Crim 2985. The judge appeared to be answering a prosecution application under gateway (c), but did not consider that the length of time was a factor. The Court of Appeal doubted whether (c) was the correct gateway, and preferred (d), but held that s.101(3) would not have barred admission.

> *jury would find it 'impossible or difficult' properly to understand other evidence in the case. The additional requirement, that its value for understanding the case as a whole is substantial, is a further hurdle for its admissibility."*[393]

Of course, gateway (c) is still subject to considerations of fairness overall, as a matter of general principle and by virtue of s.78.

Gateway (e). While ss 101(3) and (4) cannot apply to gateway (e), the Court of Appeal has indicated that the passage of time between a previous conviction and the offence charged may nonetheless "*be a very relevant matter to which the judge should draw attention when he sums up to the jury.*"[394]

Gateway (f). This does not seem to have been the subject of a time-related argument. A possible explanation is that s.105(1)(b) and s.105(3) provide different, but adequate, limitation, and the evidence is less likely to have specific probative value in correcting a false impression if the evidence is very old. Section 78 applies in general.

Gateways (d) and (g).

There are very few gateway (g) cases in which a time-related argument has been mounted. As in so many other arenas, gateway (d) takes centre stage here. However, much of the following discussion is theoretically applicable to gateway (g) cases as well, because the legislative pathway for the two gateways is identical in respect of s.101(3).

The only guidance on what length of time is enough to justify exclusion comes from the main tests for exclusion in s.101(3) and s.103(3), which are not tailored to concepts of time. Each provision only *includes* length of time as a factor that may cause the exclusionary mechanism to come into effect. Section 101(3) requires the evidence to have "*such an adverse effect on the fairness of the proceedings*". Section 103(3) requires that "*it would be unjust*" for the bad character evidence to be used to establish the defendant's propensity under s.103(1)(a). Section 103(3) is naturally

393 *Davis* [2008] EWCA Crim 1156, [2009] 2 Cr App R 17, [21].

394 *Edwards and Rowlands* [2005] EWCA Crim 3244, [2006] 2 Cr App R 4, [26].

narrower than s.101(3). Thus, while s.101(3) and (4) in particular, and s.103(3) to a lesser extent, appear to be mandatory exclusions, the interpretation of "*such an adverse effect on fairness*", "*length of time*", and "*unjust*" leaves much to the judge's discretion.[395]

A general principle is clear from *Hanson*: the passage of time does not necessarily diminish the value of bad character evidence,[396] but old convictions are likely to trigger s.101(3) unless they can show a continuing propensity.[397]

This calculation overlaps in gateway (d) cases with the first question of *Hanson*: does the history of conviction(s) establish a propensity to commit offences of the kind charged?

In *McGarvie*, the bad character evidence consisted of rape and attempted rape convictions that occurred 33 years and 18 years before a trial for rape in 2010. The Court, quashing the concviction, said: "*in our judgment, the lapse of time, 32 years since the earlier offences and 18 years since the later offence, was considerably too long to permit the admission of the convictions.*"[398] For the opposite result, see *Gillings*, where eight sexual-assault-related convictions between 1967 and 1988 were admissible at D's trial in respect of rape occurring in 2017 (a gap of 50 to 29 years). The Court said: "*This may have been an extreme case so far as the age of the convictions is concerned, but it is impossible to say that the judge's conclusions*

---

[395] Opportunities to deal with "*length of time*" include *Ullah* [2006] EWCA Crim 2003; *Jordan* [2009] EWCA Crim 953 (admitting 18-year-old foreign convictions); *BLW, RAH* [2010] EWCA Crim 1738 (where there was also an opportunity to deal with gateway (g) and s.101(3), not pursued as gateway (d) was satisfied).

[396] *Hanson* [2005] EWCA Crim 824, [2005] 2 Cr App R 21, [49], referring to the defendant's "*sexual mores and motivations*". This is evident in *Morgan* [2009] EWCA Crim 2705, where convictions for rape and indecent assault of young girls were admitted despite the offences having taken place at least 20 years earlier.

[397] *Hanson* [2005] EWCA Crim 824, [2005] 2 Cr App R 21, [11]. A period of two years since the conviction is not generally long enough, even for a young defendant: *Ceka* [2012] EWCA Crim 49. However, in *Maitland* [2005] EWCA Crim 2145 the Court excluded non-conviction bad character evidence which was 21 months old.

[398] *McGarvie* [2011] EWCA Crim 1414, [18].

were wrong."[399]

In *Murphy*, the Court of Appeal did not accept that a conviction for possession of a sawn-off shotgun 20 years earlier was capable of establishing a current propensity to commit firearms offences:

> *"There may be cases where the factual circumstances of just one conviction, even as long ago as 20 years earlier, might be relevant to showing propensity, but we would expect such cases to be rare and to be ones where the earlier conviction showed some very special and distinctive feature, such as a predilection on the part of the defendant for a highly unusual form of sexual activity, or some arcane or highly specialised knowledge relevant to the present offence."*[400]

But, in the similar case of *S*, the Court reached a different result. The defendant was convicted of robbery and of the production of a firearm, or imitation firearm, with intent to commit that robbery. Although the Court quashed the conviction for separate reasons, a secondary issue was the admission of the defendant's previous convictions (presumably under gateway (d)). There were recent convictions for a number of thefts as well as a 1988 conviction for conspiracy to rob which had involved the possession of a firearm.[401] The Court of Appeal distinguished *Murphy*:

> *"Whilst we can see that different views might be taken … about the admission of the old conviction of conspiracy to rob and possession of a firearm in the present case, it is perfectly plain to us that the situation in* Murphy *was different to this case. This was a defendant of whom it could properly be said his convictions demonstrated a propensity to steal and to use violence where necessary."*[402]

---

[399] *Gillings* [2019] EWCA Crim 1834, [2020] 2 Cr App R 8, [33].

[400] *Murphy* [2006] EWCA Crim 3408, [16]-17].

[401] *S* [2007] EWCA Crim 2105, [29]. The judgment does not appear give the year of commission of the index offences.

[402] *S* [2007] EWCA Crim 2105, [30]. *Sully* [2008] EWCA Crim 2556 also distinguished the *Murphy* principle because it only refers to limitations on using one old

This seems to be merely a matter of individual judicial discretion, unless it is really meant to be a demonstration of the intervening event principle discussed next.

5.3.3 The Intervening Event

A very old conviction may still be admissible if something has happened between that conviction and the index offence that continues the propensity.

Per the Court of Appeal in *Murphy*:

> *"In cases with less distinctive features in common, one would require some evidence of the propensity manifesting itself during the intervening period in order to render the earlier evidence admissible as evidence of a continuing propensity."*[403]

In *Cushing*, a 1989 conviction was admissible under s.103(1)(a) only because there was a similar conviction in 2004.[404] Both convictions were together capable of showing a propensity to commit the present offence of robbery. However, given that the *present* offence was also committed in 2004, it may be questioned whether the earlier 2004 conviction could really be "*evidence of propensity … during the intervening period*" and thus establish "*continuing propensity.*" Arguably, it comes too close to the present offence and too far away from the 1989 conviction. Of course, the 2004 conviction could have been admitted alone.

An easier example is *Harding*, where the Court of Appeal said that the *details* of some 1989 convictions were not significant at all, but that the convictions themselves, together with an offence committed in 1996, "*established a propensity to rob*" in 2009.[405] In *Powell*, a manslaughter in

---

conviction. In *Sully* there were two, both for indecent assaults on young girls in 1968 and 1974, which were similar enough to the present 2006 offence to be put before the jury. However, the time gap (during which the defendant had not committed any offences) was a factor in the Court of Appeal's decision to reduce sentence.

403 *Murphy* [2006] EWCA Crim 3408, [16].

404 *Cushing* [2006] EWCA Crim 1221.

405 *Harding* [2010] EWCA Crim 2145, [13].

2005 (when D was aged 17), might not by itself have been admitted at a trial for manslaughter in 2014, but when taken with two ABH offences in 2008 and 2012, established a pattern of violent offending that meant all three convictions were admissible.[406]

Caution should be exercised so as not to inadvertently bolster a weak case with bad character evidence. See, for example, *Jackson*, where a 1979 conviction and a 1989-1997 allegation were permitted as bad character evidence in respect of a 2006 trial.[407]

5.3.4 Retrospectivity

Evidence of bad character that occurred *after* the present matter can also provide sufficient continuity to avoid s.101(3).[408]

In *A*, a former police officer was convicted in 2008 of various sexual offences against his daughter. The events had taken place between 1981 and 1992, before his daughter turned 18. The bad character evidence, admitted via gateway (d), concerned the defendant's guilty plea in 2008 to making and distributing indecent photographs of children between 2005 and 2008. The judge restricted use of the conviction and the photographs to material referable to incest, and excluded the actual photos so as to reduce any prejudicial effect. He said s.101(3) was not triggered because although the material was prejudicial, it was highly relevant and powerful.

> *"In my judgment, the bad character evidence upon which the Crown seek to rely is so relevant, because it supports the proposition that* at the time the bad character evidence arose the defendant had developed *an entrenched, persistent and sustained interest in sexual offending against children, with a*

406 *Powell* [2015] EWCA Crim 2200, [11]-[18].

407 *Jackson* [2007] EWCA Crim 1892.

408 E.g. *Norris* [2013] EWCA Crim 712 (bad character evidence that occurred 20 months after the incident). See also *Richards* [2018] EWCA Crim 2374; *Adenusi* [2006] EWCA Crim 1059; *Saint* [2010] EWCA Crim 1924.

> *particular preoccupation with father/daughter incestuous sexual activity."*[409]

The prosecution argument seemed to be that the defendant's later activity indicated a developing propensity, dating back to the time of the offences against his daughter. It was also relevant that the daughter had made previous complaints to her family while the events were happening, and apparently had no knowledge of the other offences that now constituted the bad character evidence. Thus, the judge said:

> *"a reasonable jury would be entitled to consider the complainant's independent complaint and assess it in the light of the defendant's subsequent computer misuse, and conclude that the proposition that the complainant should make her complaints against an innocent man who just happened later in life to develop peculiar sexual preoccupations consistent with the complainant's complaint is profoundly unlikely."*[410]

The Court of Appeal said that incest was so abnormal and the scope of victims so narrow that the time gap was not as significant as it might be in other cases.[411] The defendant argued that if the daughter had complained immediately, the bad character evidence would not have existed at that time and so could not have prejudiced the trial. The Court of Appeal held that the judge had considered this argument under s.101(3), and, as his decision was not plainly wrong or *Wednesbury* unreasonable, appellate interference was precluded.[412]

Thus, guidelines for the treatment of retrospectivity might look something like this:

1. In general, a time gap of more than 20 years between the (alleged) commission of each offence points strongly towards exclusion under s.101(3) (and s.103(3)). The smaller the time gap (on either

409 *A* [2009] EWCA Crim 513, [16] (emphasis added).

410 *A* [2009] EWCA Crim 513, [17].

411 *A* [2009] EWCA Crim 513, [20].

412 *A* [2009] EWCA Crim 513, [22], [24].

side of the present events), the less problematic it is to attribute a propensity to the defendant at the time of the present events.

2. The time gap may be of less significance (although the court must have regard to it by the wording of sub-sections 101(3) and (4)) when the nature of the bad character evidence is so unusual that it requires the existence of special circumstances. Incest is a common example of the need for special circumstances.[413]

3. In general, *subsequent* bad character evidence, while less common, is no less admissible under the CJA. There are no temporal limits in the legislation. Nonetheless, the weight of events happening 20-25 years *after* the events in question will be very low.

4. Character is essentially the same throughout one's lifetime (barring some altering event that can be proved). In general, therefore, a person's character can be the same 25 years before the event as it is 25 years after that event. The result of this in *A* may be broadly correct, because of the type of offence concerned, but in general taking this reasoning to its logical conclusion suggests that a person is rarely likely to change at all. This is not categorically true,[414] and any use of propensity reasoning should take account of the possibility of changes in character. The onus of proving that character has not changed should rest with the prosecution, as can be seen in the above cases on intervening events.

5.3.5 Gateway (g) And The Exclusionary Provision

There are very few gateway (g) cases employing s.101(4). This may be due to the lack of purpose that gateway (g) has. Whereas the gateway (d) discussions are principally directed towards the reliability of the bad character evidence in establishing a matter in issue (usually propensity to commit the kind of offence), there is no similarly identifiable reason for

---

[413] In *D, P and U* [2011] EWCA Crim 1474, [2012] 1 Cr App R 8, [45] the Court of Appeal said, in a slightly broader context, that "*a sexual interest in young children is a characteristic which is unlikely to change over years.*"

[414] If it were, efforts in rehabilitation and restorative justice might be said to be futile.

limiting evidence admitted via gateway (g).

In *Hearne*, D was convicted of burglary. He had two previous convictions, both for burglary, in 1987 and 1997, 20 and 10 years before the present case, when he was aged 40 and 50 years respectively. In both cases he pleaded guilty. D agreed that gateway (g) was correctly triggered by his assertion that he was not committing burglary but rather rescuing illegally-kept wild birds, which was an attack on the character of C (whose business involved selling valuable birds). However, D then contended that the age of the convictions threatened the fairness of the proceedings and should be excluded under s.101(3) and (4).

The Court of Appeal held that the purpose of admission was not to demonstrate a propensity for untruthfulness, but simply as "*background*", to show the character of the person making the allegations against C.[415]

> *"The offences were, it is true, old. ...[but] It is trite that this court cannot interfere unless the response to the question of whether they should be admitted, or it was unfair to do so was outwith the range of reasonable responses. In our judgment, it was not. Plainly, as [D], fairly accepts, there had been an attack upon the character of [C] and it would have skewed the fairness of the trial had the jury been deprived of the knowledge that the source of those allegations was someone who, at a mature age, had committed burglary."*[416]

That is, "*background*" bad character evidence (especially convictions) of the defendant has no ascertainable time limits. It is not a question of judgment as to whether the evidence is sufficiently probative in some matter, it is simply a question of fact: whether the bad character evidence illustrates the background of the defendant. If it does, the lapse of time does not affect that illustration. The illustration need not be complete, or proportionate, because none of these requirements is part of the elements of gateway (g), unlike (f), (c), or even (d) (for which some amount

[415] *Hearne* [2009] EWCA Crim 103, [9].

[416] *Hearne* [2009] EWCA Crim 103, [6]. It would seem that a gap of 10 or 20 years is less significant when the defendant is of mature years, as presumably an older defendant is less likely to change in the intervening time.

of relevance needs to be established).

The result is that although the legislation provides a theoretical safeguard in s.101(3) and (4), it is not often activated with respect to gateway (g). As will be seen in the gateway (e) context below, one course of action by the courts in response to unexpectedly weak or non-existent legislative safeguards is to reinforce the strength of the primary legislative test, exercising greater rigour in its interpretation and application.[417] This has not happened in the gateway (g) context, although it would be facilitated by focusing upon the general fairness provision in s.101(3).[418] At the very least, it should be observed here that s.101(4) is intended to apply to gateway (g), and if the case law renders s.101(4) largely ineffective in relation to gateway (g), the reasoning in *Phillips* suggests we should look to other parts of the legislation, such as s.101(3), s.106, and s.101(1)(g) itself, to limit the admission of evidence via gateway (g).[419]

The exclusionary provisions still operate on evidence admitted via the *Highton* route, as to which see Chapter 4 gateway (g).

If evidence admitted via one gateway is later used for another purpose, the exclusionary provisions should be re-examined. The options when exercising s.101(3) or s.78 retrospectively upon the new usage are to (1) direct the jury to ignore the bad character evidence entirely, or (2) direct the jury to use the evidence for specified purposes only, or (3) discharge the jury.[420]

---

417 See *Phillips* [2011] EWCA Crim 2935, [2012] 1 Cr App R 25.

418 As opposed to the particular question of time specified by s.101(4).

419 *Nelson* [2006] EWCA Crim 3412 is an example of doing this, using s.101(3) to mitigate the fact that gateway (g) does not require that either the defendant or the attacked person take the stand.

420 *Henderson* [2010] EWCA Crim 1269, [2010] 2 Cr App R 24, [167] is another example of such a direction, in the context of possible gateway (d) usage when the admitting gateway was (c).

Of course, s.101(3) and s.103(3) are limited by the gateway used. Section 101(3) only applies if gateways (g) or (d) are used.[421] Neither s.101(3) nor s.103(3) can apply in the situation where the gateway is not (d) or (g), even if the usage made of the evidence is one that is traditionally associated with one of those gateways.

To fill this gap, the Court of Appeal in *Highton* relies upon s.78 of PACE. The differences between s.78 and s.101(3) are examined above. Section 78 cannot perform a pseudo-101(3) function for all gateways to which *Highton* may apply. In particular, *Highton* makes no distinction between prosecution gateways and defence gateways, but s.78 does. Therefore, presumably, evidence already admitted at the defendant's behest (e.g. via gateways (c) or (e)), can be used by the prosecution for any relevant purpose without activating any protection.[422]

5.4 Gateway (e) And The Ability To Exclude

Summary:

- There is no discretion to exclude evidence admissible under gateway (e).
- However, non-compliance with the Criminal Procedure Rules may be used to effectively 'exclude' such evidence.
- "*Substantial probative value*" means "*an enhanced capability of proving or disproving a matter in issue*".
- In the absence of a statutory limitation upon gateway (e), courts should ensure that the tests within the gateway itself are applied with greater precision and care.

---

421 Note the limited usefulness of s.101(4) for gateway (g) purposes, because whatever the age of the bad character evidence, it still tends to illustrate the defendant's background.

422 The Court has expressed "*hope*" that this would not happen: *Robinson* [2005] EWCA Crim 3233, [2006] 1 Cr App R 32.

- The assessment of substantial probative value includes the risk that the jury might become distracted from its focus on the present offence by the admission of that evidence.

The judge has no discretion to exclude evidence admitted via gateway (e), even if failure to do so would have an adverse effect on the fairness of the proceedings in respect of one co-defendant.[423]

This "*position in law is consistent with the historic rule that a defendant must be allowed to advance relevant evidence in his or her defence, even if it is damaging to a co-accused.*"[424] There is also no other residual common law principle that would allow exclusion. "*[T]he discretionary power to exclude relevant evidence which is tendered by the prosecution, if its prejudicial effect outweighs its probative value, does not apply to the position as between co-accused.*"[425]

However, there are ways around this. In *Musone*, the defendant M and co-defendant C were convicted of the murder of a fellow prisoner. A third defendant, S, was acquitted of murder on the judge's direction (but convicted of assisting M). M said that C had committed the murder. C said that he saw M with the deceased in his prison cell just after the stabbing. Both defendants had convictions involving the use of knives, but none for murder.

On the tenth day of the trial, M indicated that he wanted to adduce evidence under gateway (e) that, although acquitted some 12 years previously of an offence of murder, C had admitted (about a year before this trial) to M that in fact C was guilty of that murder.

The judge ruled that the evidence of the confession was admissible under gateway (e). The important matter in issue was whether it was C rather than M who had wielded the knife. The evidence had substantial probative value because the evidence of the confession to murder was evidence

---

423 *Land* [2006] EWCA Crim 2856; *Reid* [2006] EWCA Crim 2900, [23]; *Ferdhaus* [2010] EWCA Crim 220, [8].

424 *L* [2009] EWCA Crim 2688, [25].

425 *Apabhai* [2011] EWCA Crim 917, [27].

which was capable of showing that it was not M who stabbed the victim, but rather C. Since neither defendant had convictions for murder, if the jury accepted that C had confessed to committing murder then that was evidence which could suggest that C had killed the present victim. Moreover, the confession by C contradicted his acquittal, and might have shown a propensity to untruthfulness (s.104(1)).However, the judge held that M's failure to raise the issue earlier meant it must be excluded.

The Court of Appeal disagreed with his first reason for excluding the evidence, namely that he had an Article 6 power to ensure a fair trial. There is no express power to exclude evidence admissible under gateway (e).

However, the Court agreed with the second reason that the judge gave for excluding the evidence. Although s.111 of the CJA does not give the court power to prohibit the admission of bad character evidence where the party seeking to admit it has breached a procedural requirement, an equivalent power can be found in the *rules* made under s.111 (now Part 21, r 21.6(1) of the Criminal Procedure Rules 2020).[426] Using this power, the Court held, the judge is allowed to exclude bad character evidence in circumstances where the defendant has deliberately manipulated the trial process so as to give the co-defendant no opportunity of dealing properly with the application (as opposed to delay by mere oversight). The overriding objective of the Criminal Procedure Rules (r 1.1) is that criminal cases be dealt with justly, and each participant in the conduct of each case must conduct the case in accordance with the overriding objective (r 1.2).

> *"In our view it is not possible to see how the overriding objective can be achieved if a court has no power to prevent a deliberate manipulation of the rules by refusing to admit*

[426] *Musone* [2007] EWCA Crim 1237, [2007] 2 Cr App R 29, [56]. At the time, this was the CPR 2005 and the rule worded slightly differently, but the effect is the same and can be achieved today using CPR 2020. See also *Lawson* [2006] EWCA Crim 2572, [2007] 1 Cr App R 11.

evidence which it is sought to adduce in deliberate breach of those rules."[427]

Note that a similar point is made in the Crown Court Compendium at 12.1(2): "*When considering the admission of evidence the court must also look to its case management duties under the Crim PR and in particular r.3.2 and r.3.10. This will involve consideration of the purpose for which it is proposed to admit evidence of bad character whether by agreement or otherwise before it goes before the jury.*"[428]

Using the Rules in this way assists the court in meeting the fair trial requirement in Article 6. However, this power should only be used in circumstances where the only way in which the court can ensure fairness is by excluding such evidence. As the Court points out, these are unusual circumstances and are not likely to arise often.

They may have arisen in *Ramirez*, where D2 had volunteered, in-chief and without notice, bad character evidence about D1 in support of D2's contention that he was afraid of D1. The judge allowed this, retrospectively, because D1 was still to give evidence and could alter his case as needed. A *Musone* argument was not made, and the judge did not consider "*whether there had been a deliberate manipulation of the rules*" by the co-defendant. The Court of Appeal held that it could not replicate the judge's "*feel*" for the situation, and had no grounds upon which to conclude that D2 had deliberately manipulated the rules.[429]

The wider consequence, however, of not having a discretion to exclude evidence admitted via gateway (e), is that the gateway itself is susceptible to creative interpretations designed to perform the functions of such a discretion. This can be seen in the interpretation of "*substantial probative value*" (see discussion of *Phillips* and *Dizaei* in Chapter 5 gateway (e)).

The Court of Appeal in *Phillips* made it very clear that under the new

---

427 *Musone* [2007] EWCA Crim 1237, [2007] 2 Cr App R 29, [59].

428 Crown Court Compendium Part I: Jury and Trial Management and Summing Up.

429 *Ramirez* [2009] EWCA Crim 1721, [42].

CJA scheme,

> *"[t]he jury may … be required to make a multiplicity of judgments about a co-accused's behaviour on other occasions before reaching their conclusion as to the guilt of either defendant of the offence charged. The scope for satellite issues has significantly increased. The fairness of permitting the prosecution to introduce such issues is a factor which the judge is required to consider under section 101(1)(d) and (g) and section 101(3). No such limitation is imposed by the 2003 Act upon applications made under section 100 and section 101(1)(e). For these reasons, it is important, in our view, that sight is not lost of the rigour of the statutory test of substantial probative value upon a matter in issue between the defendants which is of substantial importance in the context of the trial as a whole."*[430]

That is, in the absence of a statutory limitation upon gateway (e), courts should ensure that the tests within the gateway itself are applied with greater precision and care.

Phillips and *Dizaei* make a significant addition to the meaning of "*probative value*". The assessment of evidential probative value has not traditionally been the sphere in which to air concerns about satellite trials. Evidence that, were it to be believed,[431] would have immense probative value may nonetheless demand a satellite trial in order to convince the jury of its truth. This does not prevent it from having probative value. That is why, where prosecution evidence is concerned and an exclusionary provision exists (such as s.101(3) or s.78), the risk of satellite litigation falls to be considered when exercising that exclusionary power, not when deciding admissibility under a relevance-based test. Yet the *Phillips* line of reasoning has, in an effort to provide a substitute-exclusionary power, included such considerations in the test for substantial probative value,

430 *Phillips* [2011] EWCA Crim 2935, [2012] 1 Cr App R 25, [40].

431 Section 109 requires that the trial judge assume this belief for the purpose of admissibility.

at least as regards defence evidence.[432]

5.5 Section 107 Stopping The Case Where Evidence Contaminated

"107 Stopping the case where evidence contaminated

(1) If on a defendant's trial before a judge and jury for an offence—

(a) evidence of his bad character has been admitted under any of paragraphs (c) to (g) of section 101(1), and

(b) the court is satisfied at any time after the close of the case for the prosecution that—

(i) the evidence is contaminated, and

(ii) the contamination is such that, considering the importance of the evidence to the case against the defendant, his conviction of the offence would be unsafe,

the court must either direct the jury to acquit the defendant of the offence or, if it considers that there ought to be a retrial, discharge the jury.

(2) Where—

(a) a jury is directed under subsection (1) to acquit a defendant of an offence, and

(b) the circumstances are such that, apart from this subsection, the defendant could if acquitted of that offence be found guilty of another offence,

the defendant may not be found guilty of that other offence if the court is satisfied as mentioned in subsection (1)(b) in respect of it.

---

432 Given its focus on the lack of exclusionary provisions for defence evidence, the Court in *Phillips* probably did not intend to suggest modifications to the existing exclusionary provisions for prosecution evidence.

(3) … [duplicate provision concerning a determination under s.4A(2) of the Criminal Procedure (Insanity) Act 1964]

(4) This section does not prejudice any other power a court may have to direct a jury to acquit a person of an offence or to discharge a jury.

(5) For the purposes of this section a person's evidence is contaminated where—

> *(a) as a result of an agreement or understanding between the person and one or more others, or*
>
> *(b) as a result of the person being aware of anything alleged by one or more others whose evidence may be, or has been, given in the proceedings,*

the evidence is false or misleading in any respect, or is different from what it would otherwise have been."

Key points:

- S.107 applies only to jury trials. It does not apply to summary trials in a magistrates' court or a *Newton* hearing.[433]
- It is in practice very limited.[434] It requires that there be "*a person's evidence*", and that this evidence be contaminated by reason of some influence by persons or evidence given (or which may be given) in the case.
- There is no formal statutory requirement that any party need *apply* for a determination under s.107.[435] As a matter of common sense, the court would be free to make a determination of its own

[433] *Bradley* [2005] EWCA Crim 20, [31].

[434] For some of the history and early discussion, see *Lamb* [2007] EWCA Crim 1766.

[435] *Woolf* [2011] EWCA Crim 2764, [31].

volition; arguably it is obliged to do so if the evidence raises the possibility of contamination.

- The test for stopping the case is whether the conviction would be unsafe—reflecting the test that the Court of Appeal would apply on appeal against conviction.
- The judge has to make a finding of fact[436] as to whether the requisite contamination has occurred. If the judge is not satisfied that it has, s.107 does not apply.
- If the judge is satisfied, the case must be stopped. There is no discretion.[437] It does not matter that there might otherwise be 'a case to answer' in the *Galbraith* sense.
- By implication, if there is merely a possibility or risk of contamination, this question should properly be left to the jury with appropriate directions.[438] In *BR*,[439] s.107 was not satisfied even though the complainants had had contact with each other and had discussed the defendant and aspects of their allegations. Contact between extended family members who are also complainants, as in this case, is "*quite typical*". The question of collusion or innocent contamination was one for a properly directed jury. The same case suggests that a financial motive or prospect of compensation to complainants does not mean that the evidence given is contaminated.
- The provision can only be used after the prosecution has closed its case.

436 See *BR* [2014] EWCA Crim 1311, [18].

437 *Card* [2006] EWCA Crim 1079, [2006] 2 Cr App R 28, [22].

438 See Chapter 6 on cross-admissibility.

439 *BR* [2014] EWCA Crim 1311, *N(H)* [2011] EWCA Crim 730.

- Failure formally to treat evidence as bad character evidence (s.107(1)(a)) does not affect the application of s.107.[440] That is, if evidence *should* have been treated as bad character evidence under s.101 gateways (c)-(g), but for whatever reason was not, an argument can still be made under s.107.

- A formal ruling from the judge is required: s.110(2)(c).

The key case on s.107 is *Card* where, unusually, the Court held that s.107 had been satisfied and the jury should have been discharged. In that case, the Court discussed the purpose behind s.107:

> *"to reduce the risk of a conviction based on over-reliance on evidence of previous misconduct and acknowledges the potential danger that, where the evidence is contaminated, the evidence of bad character may have a disproportionate impact on the evaluation of the case by the jury. In other words the dangers inherent in contamination may be obscured by the evidence of the defendant's bad character."*[441]

The successful appeal in *Card* was based on the clear contamination created by the two complainants having discussed their allegations with their mother. There was "*plain and unequivocal evidence that [C1's] evidence was different from what it would otherwise have been as a result of the conversations with her mother*". That evidence had led to a successful submission of no case to answer (second limb) in relation to C1's allegation. However, C2's allegation was left to the jury. But C2 had been present during the same conversation between C1 and the mother. The inference that C2's evidence "*was different from what it would otherwise have been if he had not been present during the same conversation … was virtually inescapable.*" The conviction was quashed.

Card proposes that, if there might be a "*responsible*" suggestion of contamination, it is better to avoid admitting any bad character evidence

[440] *Woolf* [2011] EWCA Crim 2764, [31].

[441] *Card* [2006] EWCA Crim 1079, [2006] 2 Cr App R 28, [21]. See also *King* [2008] EWCA Crim 3301.

until the suggested contaminated evidence has been examined at trial.[442] It is unclear how this should work in practice. The wording of s.107(1) suggests that the "*evidence*" in question is the "*evidence of his bad character evidence*", not the evidence in the case more generally. Thus, any allegation of contamination must be about the bad character evidence (the test in s.107(5) would seem to bear this out, as it references coincidence bad character evidence[443]). It is not clear how the contaminated evidence could be examined at trial without the bad character evidence being admitted as well.

Section 107 is not an excuse for simply repeating arguments against the admissibility of the bad character evidence. In *Renda* the Court said:

> "*We are however concerned to ensure that s.107 should not be misused. There will, of course, be occasions when counsel is justified in submitting that a conviction would be unsafe because evidence admitted under s.101(1)(c)-(g) proved to be contaminated. That however does not provide any justification for a submission which, in truth, is no more than a reiteration of the arguments advanced by counsel against the admission of this evidence. S.107 deals with a particular situation where the evidence of 'bad character' has been admitted and proves to be false or misleading in the circumstances described in s.107(5). Unless the case falls squarely within that statutory provision, the Court of Appeal Criminal Division is the appropriate venue in which the correctness of the judge's decision should be questioned.*"[444]

[442] *Card* [2006] EWCA Crim 1079, [2006] 2 Cr App R 28, [23].

[443] As to which Chapter 6 on cross-admissibility.

[444] *Renda* [2005] EWCA Crim 2826, [2006] 1 Cr App R 24, [27].

5.6 Section 108 Convictions When A Youth

"108 Offences committed by defendant when a child

(1) Section 16(2) and (3) of the Children and Young Persons Act 1963 (c. 37) (offences committed by person under 14 disregarded for purposes of evidence relating to previous convictions) shall cease to have effect.

(2) In proceedings for an offence committed or alleged to have been committed by the defendant when aged 21 or over, evidence of his conviction for an offence when under the age of 14 is not admissible unless—

> *(a) both of the offences are triable only on indictment, and*
>
> *(b) the court is satisfied that the interests of justice require the evidence to be admissible.*

(2A) Subsection (2B) applies where—

> *(a) the defendant has been convicted of an offence under the law of any country outside England and Wales ('the previous offence'), and*
>
> *(b) the previous offence would constitute an offence under the law of England and Wales ('the corresponding offence') if it were done in England and Wales at the time of the proceedings for the offence with which the defendant is now charged.*

(2B) For the purposes of subsection (2), the previous offence is to be regarded as triable only on indictment if the corresponding offence is so triable.

(3) Subsection (2) applies in addition to section 101."

Under s.108, convictions occurring before D turned 14 are not admissible against D once he turns 21, unless:

(a) both the previous conviction and the current offence are triable only on indictment, and

(b) the court is satisfied that the interests of justice require the evidence to be admissible.

The purpose of s.108 is not obvious:

> "*Quite what is the rationale behind section 108(2) is not entirely clear to us. … At all events it is possible, perhaps, to deduce that Parliament may have had in mind the period of time which might elapse between the age of 14 and the age of 21: but other than that it is difficult to draw any firm conclusions.*"[445]

In practice, most evidence that is caught by s.108 would also be likely to fall foul of s.101(3).[446]

It would appear that the action which has to have happened prior to D's 14th birthday is the "*conviction for an offence when under that age*", not "*an offence* committed *when under that age*". Thus, if the trial took place after D turned 14, s.108 would not apply.[447]

However, for a contrary view see *Assani*: "*where the person in question was under 14* at the date of the earlier incident *but over 21 at the date of the trial in which the earlier incident is potentially admissible, section 108 contains a specific restriction on admissibility*".[448] The Court assumed here that the relevant time is the date of the earlier incident, not the earlier conviction. Similar language is used in B, which refers to "*the age of the appellant [D] at the time of the misconduct alleged*".[449]

Although s.108 prima facie applies only to convictions, the Court of Appeal has said that the principle should also apply when a judge is asked

---

445 *Clark* [2014] EWCA Crim 1053, [18].

446 As in *B* [2008] EWCA Crim 1850, [17].

447 That is the implication of the language in *Hickinbottom* [2012] EWCA Crim 783, [56], where the focus is on the date of conviction.

448 *Assani* [2008] EWCA Crim 2563, [15] (emphasis added).

449 B [2008] EWCA Crim 1850, [13].

to admit evidence of misconduct which is alleged to have occurred at a time when the defendant was under the age of 14.[450]

Regardless, even if s.108 does not apply, it is obviously correct that "*judges in this context will be sensitive to an attempt to rely on previous convictions for offending which occurred when the offender was a child and in particular when the offender was a young child.*"[451]

450 *B* [2008] EWCA Crim 1850, [12].

451 *Clark* [2014] EWCA Crim 1053, [20]; the sentiment is repeated in *Valencia* [2015] EWCA Crim 857, [19].

CHAPTER SIX

JURY DIRECTIONS AND STANDARD OF PROOF

Bad character does not end with the success or failure of an argument on a pre-prepared application. The jury needs to be directed on how to use the evidence.

The Crown Court Compendium, Part 12, sets out the directions on bad character evidence.[452] Directions on cross-admissibility can be found in Part 13. These are not reproduced here.

Bad character directions should generally be given in writing.[453] They are not usually straightforward enough to be recollected by jurors afterwards.[454]

A split summing up, where directions of law are given in advance of closing speeches, is often advisable in cases involving complicated bad character points.[455]

---

452 Crown Court Compendium Part I: Jury and Trial Management and Summing Up.

453 Professor Cheryl Thomas's research in 2010 concluded that only 31% of jurors may actually understand fully their directions in the legal terms used by the judge: Cheryl Thomas, *Are Juries Fair?* (Ministry of Justice Research Series, February 2010) 38-39. This figure represents oral instructions; when written instructions were given alongside the judge's oral directions, that figure rose to nearly one-half (48%). A follow-up study in 2013, this time conducted on real jurors after the conclusion of their cases, showed an increase in the provision of written directions. This time, every one of the 70% of jurors who received them said that the written directions were helpful. Of the 30% who did not receive them, 85% said they would have preferred to have them: Cheryl Thomas, 'Avoiding the perfect storm of juror contempt' (2013) Criminal Law Review 483, 497-498. The same study showed that jurors did not welcome "*blind trust*" in their ability to deliver a proper verdict according to law; rather, they wanted better guidance on how to conduct their deliberations.

454 See *Rashid* [2019] EWCA Crim 2018.

455 *Rashid* [2019] EWCA Crim 2018.

6.1 Standard Of Proof To Be Satisfied Before Using Bad Character Evidence

Summary:

- The jury must be 'sure' that the bad character evidence is relevant in the way that the prosecution intend it to be used.

- If they are sure, they can use it to support the intended conclusion. They do not have to do so.

- In *Mitchell*-type propensity cases, where there are several instances of misconduct all tending to show a propensity, the jury does not have to be sure that each instance is proved to the criminal standard.

- The test is different when the bad character evidence is relied upon by a defendant. Where D2's bad character goes to D1's case, the jury should be directed that they must decide on a balance of probabilities ("*to what extent if at all the evidence demonstrates that it is more likely than not that the matter in issue is true*"[456]). Where the evidence goes to D2's guilt, the "*sure*" test applies.

- By inference, although it does not appear to be spelled out in the Compendium, where the jury needs to determine the truth of bad character evidence admitted at D's behest and relating to a non-defendant, the standard is the balance of probabilities.[457]

It has never been the case that the jury must be satisfied beyond reasonable doubt of the truth of every single fact upon which they rely in reaching a guilty verdict, nor is it possible to know whether the jury are so satisfied.

---

[456] See , e.g., Crown Court Compendium Part 12.7.

[457] For an example of an "*inaccurate*" direction, see *Burnett* [2016] EWCA Crim 1941, [48].

Early CJA cases adopted the "*sure*" wording, importing the standard of proof of beyond reasonable doubt. The judge in *Crandle* instructed: "*If you are* less than sure *about those matters, then you must disregard the convictions entirely because they will then have no probative value at all.*"[458] This is essentially the same as in *Lafayette*:

> *"An allegation of 'reprehensible behaviour' will normally be admissible (see section 109), but unless the jury* are sure *that the appellant engaged in the alleged reprehensible behaviour, they cannot rely on it for the purposes of assessing the defendant's credibility or his propensity to commit offences of the kind with which he is charged."*[459]

The Court of Appeal in *Vickers* even required that this standard be satisfied for the facts underlying a conviction. Not only should the jury "*be sure*" that the previous convictions demonstrated the propensity in question, but "*they had to be sure about the facts underlying one of those convictions before they acted upon it.*"[460]

Z focuses on the quality of the evidence. In that case the judge failed to make this standard clear, and this was one ground that led to the conviction being overturned.

> *"[S]ince it was sought to admit it as evidence of bad character, it had to be sufficiently cogent for a reasonable jury to be able to be sure of its truth. Thus, if the judge was minded to admit the evidence under section 101, he had then to consider whether the jury would reasonably be able to be sure of its truth. … the judge in his summing up did not make it clear to the jury that this evidence could be taken into account only if they were sure of the truth of Mrs Z's allegation."*[461]

In *Ngyuen*, although the Court stated that jurors do not "*all have to travel*

458 *Crandle* [2006] EWCA Crim 2663, [30] (emphasis added).

459 *Lafayette* [2008] EWCA Crim 3238, [37] (emphasis added).

460 *Vickers* [2012] EWCA Crim 2689, [37].

461 *Z* [2009] EWCA Crim 20, [2009] 1 Cr App R 34, [27].

down the same evidential route",[462] it was nonetheless necessary that they be satisfied to the criminal standard of proof before relying on bad character evidence as establishing propensity.[463]

The definitive statement is now from the Supreme Court decision in *Mitchell.* That case tells us:

- The existence of a propensity must be proved to the conventional criminal standard.[464] I.e., the jury need to be sure that the propensity has been proved.
- In *Ngyuen*, the only way in which they could be sure was by being convinced that the sole incident said to show propensity had been proved to the criminal standard.
- However, in cases where there are several instances of misconduct, all tending to show a propensity, the jury do *not* have to be convinced of the truth and accuracy of all aspects of each of those.
- Rather, the jury should allow the individual instances to "*inform*" each other, in assessing whether they are sure propensity exists "*in the round*".
- "*[J]urors are at liberty to follow their own evidential track.*" Individual jurors may be sure that a propensity exists and then take it into account in deciding their individual verdict. The jury as a whole does not need to agree that a propensity exists before some jurors can use it.

It might be said that this standard of proof increases the risk of satellite litigation. *McKenzie* said that proof of previous alleged misconduct (i.e. not via a conviction) "*requires the trial of a collateral or satellite issue*".[465]

---

462 *Ngyuen* [2008] EWCA Crim 585, [2008] 2 Cr App R 9, [30].

463 *Ngyuen* [2008] EWCA Crim 585, [2008] 2 Cr App R 9, [29].

464 *Mitchell* [2016] UKSC 55, [2017] AC 571, [44].

465 *McKenzie* [2008] EWCA Crim 758, [23].

Mitchell states that the avoidance of satellite litigation is one reason for not applying the criminal standard to each instance of bad character.[466] In analysing *O'Dowd*[467] the Supreme Court stated: "*The jury should have been directed to consider whether the sum of that evidence established to the criminal standard that the defendant was possessed of the propensity which was alleged. The evidence in relation to those incidents should have been considered cumulatively, not as separate aspects of the case for a propensity, isolated one from the other.*"[468]

When modifying a good character direction, the Crown Court Compendium states that:[469]

"*where the prosecution relies on disputed evidence of previous misconduct on the part of a defendant otherwise entitled to a good character direction, the judge should direct the jury that:*

> *(1) if they are sure the evidence is true, they may take it into account as evidence of bad character, adding an appropriate bad character direction; whereas*
>
> *(2) if they are not sure the evidence is true, they should disregard it, adding an appropriate good character direction.*"

This direction imports a requirement of "*sure*" into the jury's decision.

A failure properly to direct the jury as to standard of proof is not fatal. In *Dalby*, the Court of Appeal agreed that the judge had failed to give a direction that the jury needed to be sure of the truth of the bad character evidence before they could rely upon it.[470] However, the Court was satisfied that the conviction was safe, because "*the substance of the [bad character] evidence was admitted in the course of the appellant's evidence. That is a significant factor in reducing the impact of the failure to give a direction*

[466] *Mitchell* [2016] UKSC 55, [2017] AC 571, [47].

[467] *O'Dowd* [2009] EWCA Crim 905, [2009] 2 Cr App R 16.

[468] *Mitchell* [2016] UKSC 55, [2017] AC 571, [52].

[469] Part 11. See Chapter 2 for good character.

[470] *Dalby* [2012] EWCA Crim 701, [23].

that the jury needed to be sure of the truth of that evidence before they could rely upon it."[471] That is, the fact that much of the bad character evidence was accepted by the defendant meant that for practical purposes the jury did not need to make a finding on the truth of those parts, and it was those parts of the evidence that were significant for bad character purposes. This could not, presumably, work if the prosecution was relying upon a part of the evidence that was not agreed.

In *Styles*, even giving a bad character direction where one should not have been given, and failing to give a modified good character direction where it should have been given, was not sufficient to render the conviction unsafe.[472] Contrast *Greenwood*, where in somewhat similar circumstances the conviction was quashed.[473]

There are cases where (along with other successful grounds of appeal) failure to give the correct direction has resulted in a conviction being quashed.[474]

6.2 The Safety Valve

Summary:

- Jury directions can protect against the erroneous use, or misuse, of bad character evidence: the "*safety valve*".
- Failure to give proper directions is not fatal to a conviction.

In many cases where the judge has or may have made an error in applying the CJA, the Court of Appeal has often relied upon "*safety valve*"[475] of

[471] *Dalby* [2012] EWCA Crim 701, [24].

[472] *Styles* [2015] EWCA Crim 1619, [35]-[36].

[473] *Greenwood* [2012] EWCA Crim 3147, [14].

[474] *Hackett* [2019] EWCA Crim 983; *Harty* [2016] EWCA Crim 345.

[475] *Eastlake* [2007] EWCA Crim 603, [26]. See also *Culhane* [2006] EWCA Crim 1053; *Isichei* [2006] EWCA Crim 1815; *Osbourne* [2007] EWCA Crim 481; *RR* [2007] EWCA Crim 437; *Saleem* [2007] EWCA Crim 1923; *Tirnaveanu* [2007] EWCA Crim 1239, [2007] 2 Cr App R 23; *Walker* [2007] EWCA Crim 2631, [2008] 2 Cr App R

jury directions.

This phrase was first employed in this context in *Eastlake*. Brothers Scott and Nicky were convicted of assault charges. The issue was identification. Bad character evidence about both was admitted via gateway (d): Scott had four convictions relating to street violence between 2003-04; Nicky had a conviction for an assault in 2004, and another for an offence (committed with Scott) in 2004. The defendants' opposition to admission was based on the weakness of the prosecution case, which was based solely upon one witness's identification of the defendants. The judge accepted that there was

> *"some force in those submissions. However, I am conscious that the Judicial Studies Board guideline for directing a jury about bad character is a very strong one and I am satisfied, having given the jury a direction on identification and the dangers thereto and the new guideline direction on bad character, that the jury would properly be able to assess the strength of the identification without injustice to the defendants."*[476]

The Court of Appeal went further—it felt that this was not a weak case, and that in any event the dangers of using bad character evidence in such circumstances were mitigated by jury directions:

> *"This case exemplifies the paradox inherent in the admission of bad character evidence of this sort. The previous convictions were of recent date and for offences similar to (albeit less serious than) those charged in this indictment. The more recent and similar the previous convictions are, the more powerfully they may indicate a relevant propensity; but those factors may strengthen the argument that they should be excluded to avoid the risk of the trial becoming unbalanced by their admission into evidence.*

(S) 6; *Lamaletie and Royce* [2008] EWCA Crim 314; *Laurusevicius* [2008] EWCA Crim 3020; *Brisland* [2008] EWCA Crim 2773; *Foster* [2009] EWCA Crim 353; *X* [2012] EWCA Crim 2276.

[476] *Eastlake* [2007] EWCA Crim 603, [15].

> *The* safety valve *is of course the giving of proper directions to the jury."*[477]

The parties did not dispute that the judge gave the proper directions in this case.

The safety valve is therefore another way of dealing with potential unfairness or adverse effect of admitting bad character evidence. It should be approached with caution, because it can skirt a fine line between a case that actually invites exclusion under s.78, s.101(3), or s.103(3), and a case where the evidence is properly admissible but requires clear instructions as to its limitations.[478]

However, the absence of the correct jury direction does not therefore render a conviction *unsafe*.[479] The Court of Appeal in *Ahmed*[480] agreed that the directions were "*scrappy*". However, the prosecution case was strong, and the previous convictions "*plainly demonstrated a relevant propensity.*"

In *Girma*, evidence of the convictions of non-defendants was admitted via s.74 of PACE (and, wrongly, gateway (c)). When admitting the evidence, the judge "*said he would give a careful direction to the jury that they could not use the convictions to bolster the present case.*"[481] As to the later failure to do this:

> *"In the event, he said nothing about [the convictions]. No-one invited him to do so.*
>
> *"As it seems to us, this is wholly peripheral. It may be (and it is unnecessary to decide) that absent agreement by the*

---

[477] *Eastlake* [2007] EWCA Crim 603, [25]-[26] (emphasis added).

[478] See, e.g., the unusual set of events in *Wilson* [2008] EWCA Crim 134, [2008] 2 Cr App R 3.

[479] See also *Brisland* [2008] EWCA Crim 2773, [23]. For a failure to direct on usage when the issue is as complex as the cross-admissibility of several counts in the same trial see *Francis-Macrae* [2006] EWCA Crim 2635.

[480] *Ahmed* [2011] EWCA Crim 3253, [11].

[481] The convictions, of alleged co-offenders, had both positive and negative implications for various defendants in the present trial.

> *defendants, this was irrelevant evidence which should not have been admitted. However, its admission could not conceivably have prejudiced these appellants. It could not conceivably affect the safety of the convictions. We need say no more about it."*[482]

In this case the strength of the evidence meant that the Court was not unduly concerned that non-defendant bad character, admitted via the wrong legislative path, had been left to the jury without direction as to its use or scope.

In the complex and lengthy case of *Tirnaveanu*, the Court said that there was no serious error in the judge's failure to direct as to usage. "*[T]here can be little doubt that at the end of a trial extending over two months the jury had at the forefront of their minds the relevance of the other evidence and the use they could make of it.*"[483]

It might be concluded, therefore, that directions to the jury on the use of bad character evidence are in principle required, in practice useful, but not always necessary. This is so despite the pivotal statement in *Edwards and Rowlands* that jury directions are of "*the first importance*".[484]

Note that accidental or erroneous reference to bad character can sometimes be remedied by a warning to the jury to ignore the material.[485]

Thus, where proper directions are given they may be capable of saving the day (the safety valve in operation), but if the valve is 'off' the case may nonetheless be safe. Of course, a case may be safe without the operation of the valve—most commonly because the evidence against the defendant was so strong that the jury would nonetheless have convicted.

---

482 *Girma* [2009] EWCA Crim 912, [2010] 1 Cr App R (S) 28, [84]-[85].

483 *Tirnaveanu* [2007] EWCA Crim 1239, [2007] 2 Cr App R 23, [37]. See also, recently, *Heron* [2020] EWCA Crim 966.

484 *Edwards and Rowlands* [2005] EWCA Crim 3244, [2006] 2 Cr App R 4.

485 *Burchell* [2016] EWCA Crim 1559, [32]; *Kelly* [2015] EWCA Crim 500.

6.3 Are Juries Influenced By Bad Character Evidence?

The jury's actual use of bad character evidence cannot easily be studied. Nor can the effect of jury directions on the use of that evidence. Some guidance is available by looking at retrials that used different evidence, and research and mock-trials.[486]

Bad character evidence has occasionally been introduced for the first time in a *re*trial, allowing some comparison with the first trial. These cases are of limited value because it cannot be known what factors influenced each jury in each trial, nor what differences existed within each jury room. But they are at least suggestive of how a jury may receive bad character evidence, indicating that juries are quite likely to be influenced by bad character evidence.

Benguit involved three trials (thus two retrials) of the defendant for killing a woman by stabbing. He was convicted at the third trial, the first two juries being unable to agree.

In both retrials, the judge allowed evidence from two new witnesses that suggested the defendant had a propensity to carry a knife. Only one of the new witnesses was called at the first retrial, but she "*behaved in such a way that it was considered appropriate to discharge her from giving evidence before she had referred to the matter of the knife.*"[487] She was recalled at the second retrial, where the prosecution also called the second witness. The first witness said she had been inside a house with the defendant and he had a knife. The second witness said that he saw the defendant in the bay window of a house appearing to sharpen the blade of a knife. Neither witness could recall exactly when they saw this. It is not known whether both witnesses were referring to the same house. In any case, the murder took place on a public road.

It is revealing that the evidence was apparently used only as a last resort. The prosecution had not sought to put the evidence before the first jury (although it was available), had sought to put the evidence of only one

[486] See, e.g., studies by Sally Lloyd-Bostock and Cheryl Thomas.

[487] *Benguit* [2005] EWCA Crim 1953, [17]-[19]. See also *Urushadze* [2008] EWCA Crim 2498; *Brand* [2009] EWCA Crim 2878.

witness before the second jury, and only in the third trial were both witnesses used.

The third jury could not have known of the prosecution's selectiveness, but the judge did. Should this have been taken into account under s.101(3)?[488] It is interesting that the conviction came only after this extra evidence—as if it was necessary (given the weakness of the other evidence in the case) for the defendant to have some propensity before the jury were satisfied. Was the evidence merely the probative tipping-point, or was it of such little assistance that the prosecution did not want to use it in the first place?

In *T* the defendant was convicted, on retrial, of nine sexual offences against two boys; he was acquitted on a tenth count.[489]

The events in relation to each boy occurred separately. The bad character evidence came from three other boys who each said that the defendant had behaved improperly with them (each on a separate occasion). These were uncharged events. Two of these boys testified at the first trial; at retrial the third also gave evidence. His allegation was far more serious than the other two uncharged allegations.[490] The judge also admitted a substantial body of evidence to support the uncharged acts, mainly from people to whom each boy had complained. The defendant did not challenge the admission of these uncharged allegations, and so it did not become clear why the third allegation was not used in the first trial. Whatever the reason, the admission of the third allegation as bad character evidence may well have contributed to the conviction on retrial. The charged events for which the defendant was convicted consisted of genital touching, mutual masturbation, and oral sex. The first two uncharged allegations were that, in each case, the defendant had stroked the stomach and inside the waistband of the boy's lower clothing, without touching

[488] Section 101(3) was not considered at the second retrial because the judge, applying common law rules, held that the evidence was relevant and probative, and that its probative value outweighed its prejudicial effect. The Court of Appeal held that the evidence was in fact correctly admissible under s.101(1)(d) and the judge had impliedly dealt with s.101(3) (at [32]).

[489] A second retrial was later ordered due to a defect in the bad character directions.

[490] *T* [2008] EWCA Crim 484, [6]-[9].

the genitals. In contrast, the third uncharged allegation was that the defendant had touched his genitals and masturbated him. This allegation bears much more similarity to the charged events and, it could be argued, would have greater probative value in relation to establishing a propensity. If so, it is perhaps an appropriate outcome that the less similar allegations did not persuade the jury, but that the similarity of the third allegation was enough to indicate true propensity. On the other hand, it is possible that it took the combined efforts of all three pieces of evidence to create such convincing evidence of propensity.

In *Campbell*[491] the bad character evidence appears to have had little impact of its own accord. The defendant was convicted at both the original trial and the retrial, although the evidence of his previous convictions for the same type of offence was adduced only at the retrial (ordered due to deficiencies in the summing up). A possible suggestion is that the non-bad character evidence was independently strong enough to secure a conviction.

Of course, any conclusion that can be drawn from these retrials is subject to the caveat that we do not know how every piece of evidence was presented at the original trial compared with the retrial, and what other factors may have influenced the jury. Practitioners will have cases where a client's bad character has been admitted and an acquittal secured. Character is no substitute for the facts of the incident and may mean much less to the jury than it does to the prosecution or defendant. But the available material suggests that is not a negligible or trivial factor in jury deliberations.

6.4 Cross-Admissibility

Section 112(2) reads:

"Where a defendant is charged with two or more offences in the same criminal proceedings, this Chapter (except section 101(3)) has effect as if each offence

[491] *Campbell* [2006] EWCA Crim 1305.

were charged in separate proceedings; and references to the offence with which the defendant is charged are to be read accordingly."

The effect of s.112(2) is that evidence in relation to count 1 on the indictment, and in fact a conviction on count 1 itself, can only be used by the jury in relation to count 2 if count 1 and its evidence satisfy a s.101 gateway.

As a result, the notice provisions apply (see Chapter 2).

Cross-admissibility must be addressed by the judge with counsel well in advance of any directions and closing speeches. Raising the point on the first day of summing-up is "*not a helpful way to proceed*".[492]

In practice, the cross-admissibility direction is often given as a matter of course. Gateway (d) cross-admissibility generally applies to the following categories:[493]

(1) Coincidence approach. When independent but similar complaints are made against the same person, the jury "*may be permitted to consider the improbability that those complaints are the product of mere coincidence or malice*". This means that C1's evidence on count 1 can be relevant to C2's credibility on count 2. This is an important matter in issue: s.101(1)(d)). Jurors first need to exclude any collusion/innocent contamination between the similar complaints.[494]

(2) Propensity approach. The jury may be sure of D's guilt upon count 1, and if, but only if, they are also sure that guilt on count 1 establishes D's propensity to commit that kind of offence, they may proceed to consider whether the propensity makes it more likely that D committed an offence of a similar type alleged in

492 *Gabbai* [2019] EWCA Crim 2287, [2020] 4 WLR 65, [83]-[87]. See also *Adams* [2019] EWCA Crim 1363.

493 *N(H)* [2011] EWCA Crim 730, [31].

494 See, e.g., *Smith* [2017] EWCA Crim 941, [28].

count 2 on the same indictment (evidence of propensity: section 101(1)(d) and section 103(1)(a)).

The first category is described as the "*coincidence approach*". It is effectively the same as what used to be known as "*pooling*" evidence in pre-CJA commentary. The second category is described as the "*propensity*" approach, which is akin to "*sequential*" evidence in the pre-CJA commentary.

It is rare that both of the above categories will apply to the same counts. In most cases, this would be impermissible bootstrapping: (a) using the similarity of the two complaints on counts 1 and 2 to reach a verdict of guilty on count 1 (the coincidence approach), and then (b) using that guilty verdict to support a guilty finding on count 2 (the propensity approach). The evidence in relation to count 2 having already been used in step (a), it should not be used in step (b) as this would effectively give that evidence twice the weight it should have. A glance at the specimen direction in the Compendium shows just how difficult it is to overcome this problem and why this combination should be used very sparingly.

Note that the exception in s.101(3) cannot apply, because the effect would be to exclude the evidence in question from the trial and create a severed indictment.[495] For the same reason, presumably s.103(3) and s.78 cannot apply (although s.78 can still apply on general grounds).

For a case where cross-admissibility of different counts should not have been permitted, see *Gabbai*. There, although the relevant counts all alleged rape, they were materially different on the alleged facts and issues in dispute. C1's allegation was based on the removal of a condom during otherwise consensual sex, whilst she was in a relationship with D. C2's allegation was of extreme violence and forced penetration by D, a complete stranger.

> *"In this way the two instances are entirely dissimilar. In our view, whether viewed through the prism of coincidence or propensity, [C1's] allegation could not logically assist the jury with whether [C2]*

[495] For a case where severance and the effect of bad character and cross-admissibility is examined, see *Toner* [2019] EWCA Crim 447.

> *had consented to rough sex (or anal penetration), just as [C2's] allegation could not assist the jury with the issue of whether [C1] had, on the relevant occasion, consented to sex without a condom. In our judgment, the jury was not entitled to find the counts mutually reinforcing. The similarity advanced was on the very limited basis that during rough sex the appellant went further than the complainant wanted. The suggested propensity was, as the prosecution had put it, 'losing control in the moment and/or exploiting his physical, dominant role in the sexual activity, paying little or no regard to the wishes of his sexual partner'. Each case turns upon its facts and the facts here were too widely distinct for cross-admissibility be left to the jury."*[496]

The prejudicial effect of cross-admissibility in this case was so high that, taken together with other "*aspects of this trial which went awry*", the convictions were unsafe.

Failure to give the cross-admissibility direction is likely to cast doubt on the safety of a conviction. The Court of Appeal in *Adams* issued the following general reminder:

> *"Looking at the matter more broadly, the general tendency of the criminal law over time has been towards a gradual relaxation of rules of evidence and an increasing willingness to trust to the good sense and rationality of juries to judge for themselves whether particular evidence is relevant to an issue they have to decide and if so in what way. But we have not yet reached the point where evidence of a defendant's bad character can be left as a free for all. The particular ways in which evidence that a person has committed one offence may or may not be relevant in deciding whether that person is guilty of another offence are not always immediately obvious even to legal professionals and have had to be worked out by the courts in a number of cases. Lay jurors are entitled to assistance on these questions and cannot be expected to work out the approach which the courts regard as proper for themselves. It therefore seems to us to be essential that, in a case of this kind, the jury should be given clear directions on*

[496] *Gabbai* [2019] EWCA Crim 2287, [2020] 4 WLR 65, [81]-[82].

> *whether, and if so how, evidence relating to one count may be taken into account in deciding guilt on another count.*[497]

Wrongful inclusion of a summary charge on the indictment does not necessarily render a conviction on the indictable count unsafe. In *Morris*, the evidence covered by the summary charge was treated as s.98(a) evidence in relation to the indictable counts.[498]

[497] *Adams* [2019] EWCA Crim 1363, [22].

[498] *Morris* [2019] EWCA Crim 147.

CHAPTER SEVEN

CONCLUSION

It would be ideal if there was a simple crib-sheet or flowchart to help navigate the bad character provisions of the CJA. In the absence of such miracles, the following steps may help.

Preliminary:

- Is it fair to use this evidence in this case?
- Particularly if prosecuting, how does it actually help the tribunal of fact to ascertain the truth (as opposed to making one's own case stronger)?
- Does it distract the parties, the judge, or the jury from the issues that must be resolved in the case?
- If an error is made in respect of the admission or directions on the evidence, how might this affect the safety of any subsequent conviction?

If seeking to use bad character evidence:

- Has the appropriate notice/application been made?
- Does the evidence meet the requirements of a gateway?
- Are there reasons why the judge might be concerned about the evidence or the gateway?
- Which other parties may be affected by the evidence?
- Can the judge direct the jury appropriately on the use of the evidence?
- Do any exclusions or pseudo-exclusions apply?

The law on bad character is still developing and changing. While the flurry of appellate decisions from the first 10 years has quietened, new judgments are still being handed down regularly. Occasionally, these explain complications that have not previously been resolved. Sometimes, they patch over inconsistencies or illogicalities in the legislation. At other times, they remedy an error of application or interpretation that has been dealt with in previous cases. The wealth of primary material that has informed this book shows just how much complexity can be created by a handful of provisions that were intended to usher in a more straightforward approach to character.

INDEX

MORE BOOKS BY LAW BRIEF PUBLISHING

A selection of our other titles available now:-

'A Practical Guide to Solicitor and Client Costs – 2nd Edition' by Robin Dunne
'Constructive Dismissal – Practice Pointers and Principles' by Benjimin Burgher
'A Practical Guide to Religion and Belief Discrimination Claims in the Workplace' by Kashif Ali
'A Practical Guide to the Law of Medical Treatment Decisions' by Ben Troke
'Fundamental Dishonesty and QOCS in Personal Injury Proceedings: Law and Practice' by Jake Rowley
'A Practical Guide to the Law in Relation to School Exclusions' by Charlotte Hadfield & Alice de Coverley
'A Practical Guide to Divorce for the Silver Separators' by Karin Walker
'The Right to be Forgotten – The Law and Practical Issues' by Melissa Stock
'A Practical Guide to Planning Law and Rights of Way in National Parks, the Broads and AONBs' by James Maurici QC, James Neill et al
'A Practical Guide to Election Law' by Tom Tabori
'A Practical Guide to the Law in Relation to Surrogacy' by Andrew Powell
'A Practical Guide to Claims Arising from Fatal Accidents – 2nd Edition' by James Patience
'A Practical Guide to the Ownership of Employee Inventions – From Entitlement to Compensation' by James Tumbridge & Ashley Roughton
'A Practical Guide to Asbestos Claims' by Jonathan Owen & Gareth McAloon
'A Practical Guide to Stamp Duty Land Tax in England and Northern Ireland' by Suzanne O'Hara
'A Practical Guide to the Law of Farming Partnerships' by Philip Whitcomb

'Covid-19, Homeworking and the Law – The Essential Guide to Employment and GDPR Issues' by Forbes Solicitors
'Covid-19, Force Majeure and Frustration of Contracts – The Essential Guide' by Keith Markham
'Covid-19 and Criminal Law – The Essential Guide' by Ramya Nagesh
'Covid-19 and Family Law in England and Wales – The Essential Guide' by Safda Mahmood
'A Practical Guide to the Law of Unlawful Eviction and Harassment – 2nd Edition' by Stephanie Lovegrove
'Covid-19, Residential Property, Equity Release and Enfranchisement – The Essential Guide' by Paul Sams and Louise Uphill
'Covid-19, Brexit and the Law of Commercial Leases – The Essential Guide' by Mark Shelton
'A Practical Guide to Costs in Personal Injury Claims – 2nd Edition' by Matthew Hoe
'A Practical Guide to the General Data Protection Regulation (GDPR) – 2nd Edition' by Keith Markham
'Ellis on Credit Hire – Sixth Edition' by Aidan Ellis & Tim Kevan
'A Practical Guide to Working with Litigants in Person and McKenzie Friends in Family Cases' by Stuart Barlow
'Protecting Unregistered Brands: A Practical Guide to the Law of Passing Off' by Lorna Brazell
'A Practical Guide to Secondary Liability and Joint Enterprise Post-Jogee' by Joanne Cecil & James Mehigan
'A Practical Guide to the Pre-Action RTA Claims Protocol for Personal Injury Lawyers' by Antonia Ford
'A Practical Guide to Neighbour Disputes and the Law' by Alexander Walsh
'A Practical Guide to Forfeiture of Leases' by Mark Shelton
'A Practical Guide to Coercive Control for Legal Practitioners and Victims' by Rachel Horman

'A Practical Guide to Rights Over Airspace and Subsoil' by Daniel Gatty
'Tackling Disclosure in the Criminal Courts – A Practitioner's Guide' by Narita Bahra QC & Don Ramble
'A Practical Guide to the Law of Driverless Cars – Second Edition' by Alex Glassbrook, Emma Northey & Scarlett Milligan
'A Practical Guide to TOLATA Claims' by Greg Williams
'Artificial Intelligence – The Practical Legal Issues' by John Buyers
'A Practical Guide to the Law of Prescription in Scotland' by Andrew Foyle
'A Practical Guide to the Construction and Rectification of Wills and Trust Instruments' by Edward Hewitt
'A Practical Guide to the Law of Bullying and Harassment in the Workplace' by Philip Hyland
'How to Be a Freelance Solicitor: A Practical Guide to the SRA-Regulated Freelance Solicitor Model' by Paul Bennett
'A Practical Guide to Prison Injury Claims' by Malcolm Johnson
'A Practical Guide to the Small Claims Track' by Dominic Bright
'A Practical Guide to Advising Clients at the Police Station' by Colin Stephen McKeown-Beaumont
'A Practical Guide to Antisocial Behaviour Injunctions' by Iain Wightwick
'Practical Mediation: A Guide for Mediators, Advocates, Advisers, Lawyers, and Students in Civil, Commercial, Business, Property, Workplace, and Employment Cases' by Jonathan Dingle with John Sephton
'The Mini-Pupillage Workbook' by David Boyle
'A Practical Guide to Crofting Law' by Brian Inkster
'A Practical Guide to Spousal Maintenance' by Liz Cowell
'A Practical Guide to the Law of Domain Names and Cybersquatting' by Andrew Clemson
'A Practical Guide to the Law of Gender Pay Gap Reporting' by Harini Iyengar

'A Practical Guide to the Rights of Grandparents in Children Proceedings' by Stuart Barlow
'NHS Whistleblowing and the Law' by Joseph England
'Employment Law and the Gig Economy' by Nigel Mackay & Annie Powell
'A Practical Guide to Noise Induced Hearing Loss (NIHL) Claims' by Andrew Mckie, Ian Skeate, Gareth McAloon
'An Introduction to Beauty Negligence Claims – A Practical Guide for the Personal Injury Practitioner' by Greg Almond
'Intercompany Agreements for Transfer Pricing Compliance' by Paul Sutton
'Zen and the Art of Mediation' by Martin Plowman
'A Practical Guide to the SRA Principles, Individual and Law Firm Codes of Conduct 2019 – What Every Law Firm Needs to Know' by Paul Bennett
'A Practical Guide to Adoption for Family Lawyers' by Graham Pegg
'A Practical Guide to Industrial Disease Claims' by Andrew Mckie & Ian Skeate
'A Practical Guide to Redundancy' by Philip Hyland
'A Practical Guide to Vicarious Liability' by Mariel Irvine
'A Practical Guide to Applications for Landlord's Consent and Variation of Leases' by Mark Shelton
'A Practical Guide to Relief from Sanctions Post-Mitchell and Denton' by Peter Causton
'A Practical Guide to Equity Release for Advisors' by Paul Sams
'A Practical Guide to the Law Relating to Food' by Ian Thomas
'A Practical Guide to Financial Services Claims' by Chris Hegarty
'The Law of Houses in Multiple Occupation: A Practical Guide to HMO Proceedings' by Julian Hunt
'A Practical Guide to Unlawful Eviction and Harassment' by Stephanie Lovegrove
'Occupiers, Highways and Defective Premises Claims: A Practical Guide Post-Jackson – 2nd Edition' by Andrew Mckie

'A Practical Guide to Financial Ombudsman Service Claims' by Adam Temple & Robert Scrivenor
'A Practical Guide to Advising Schools on Employment Law' by Jonathan Holden
'A Practical Guide to Running Housing Disrepair and Cavity Wall Claims: 2nd Edition' by Andrew Mckie & Ian Skeate
'A Practical Guide to Holiday Sickness Claims – 2nd Edition' by Andrew Mckie & Ian Skeate
'Arguments and Tactics for Personal Injury and Clinical Negligence Claims' by Dorian Williams
'A Practical Guide to Drone Law' by Rufus Ballaster, Andrew Firman, Eleanor Clot
'A Practical Guide to Compliance for Personal Injury Firms Working With Claims Management Companies' by Paul Bennett
'A Practical Guide to Dog Law for Owners and Others' by Andrea Pitt
'RTA Allegations of Fraud in a Post-Jackson Era: The Handbook – 2nd Edition' by Andrew Mckie
'RTA Personal Injury Claims: A Practical Guide Post-Jackson' by Andrew Mckie
'On Experts: CPR35 for Lawyers and Experts' by David Boyle
'An Introduction to Personal Injury Law' by David Boyle
'A Practical Guide to Subtle Brain Injury Claims' by Pankaj Madan

These books and more are available to order online direct from the publisher at www.lawbriefpublishing.com, where you can also read free sample chapters. For any queries, contact us on 0844 587 2383 or mail@lawbriefpublishing.com.

Our books are also usually in stock at www.amazon.co.uk with free next day delivery for Prime members, and at good legal bookshops such as Wildy & Sons.

We are regularly launching new books in our series of practical day-to-day practitioners' guides. Visit our website and join our free newsletter to be kept informed and to receive special offers, free chapters, etc.

You can also follow us on Twitter at www.twitter.com/lawbriefpub.

www.ingramcontent.com/pod-product-compliance
Lightning Source LLC
LaVergne TN
LVHW052316200926
848481LV00002B/579
9781913715267